THE MARKETING MACHINE

HOW TO ENGINEER PROFITABLE, EFFECTIVE MARKETING FOR YOUR SMALL BUSINESS

ROS CONKIE

For Paul, Nathaniel and Bella

CONTENTS

IGNITION

When my grandmother completed her engineering degree in the 1930s, she was one of only two women on her entire course. Most people told her she didn't belong — women, they said, weren't meant to be engineers. But Sheila McGuffie wasn't one to be told she couldn't do something, and she proved those people wrong. She went on to work on one of the most creative and revolutionary inventions of the twentieth century: the jet engine. She helped shape the future of aviation, transforming how we travel and connect with the world.

At a time when women were often overlooked and disregarded, she helped design and test a machine that could harness invisible forces — airflow, pressure, and combustion — and turn them into something powerful enough to change the world.

Working with Sir Frank Whittle and his visionary team, she tested, tweaked, and refined until they had a machine that worked perfectly.

In a way, marketing has a similar challenge. Businesses must harness invisible forces — like customer emotions, desires, and decision-making processes — and turn them into something powerful and predictable. Achieving this isn't about guesswork or luck. It's about applying creativity with precision, building systems that can be tested and improved until they deliver consistent results.

My grandmother's story has always inspired me, not just because of what she achieved, but because of how she achieved it. Great engineering combines creativity with discipline. It requires an understanding of the materials and forces at play, a clear vision for the desired outcome, and a willingness to iterate until every part works together perfectly.

This book is about applying those same principles to marketing. It's about creating a machine — a marketing machine — that reliably generates loyal customers. Like the jet engine, it will require careful design and fine-tuning. Unlike a jet engine, you don't need an engineering degree to understand it! And once it's built, it will transform your business, enabling you to reach new heights and accelerate your growth.

Let's get started.

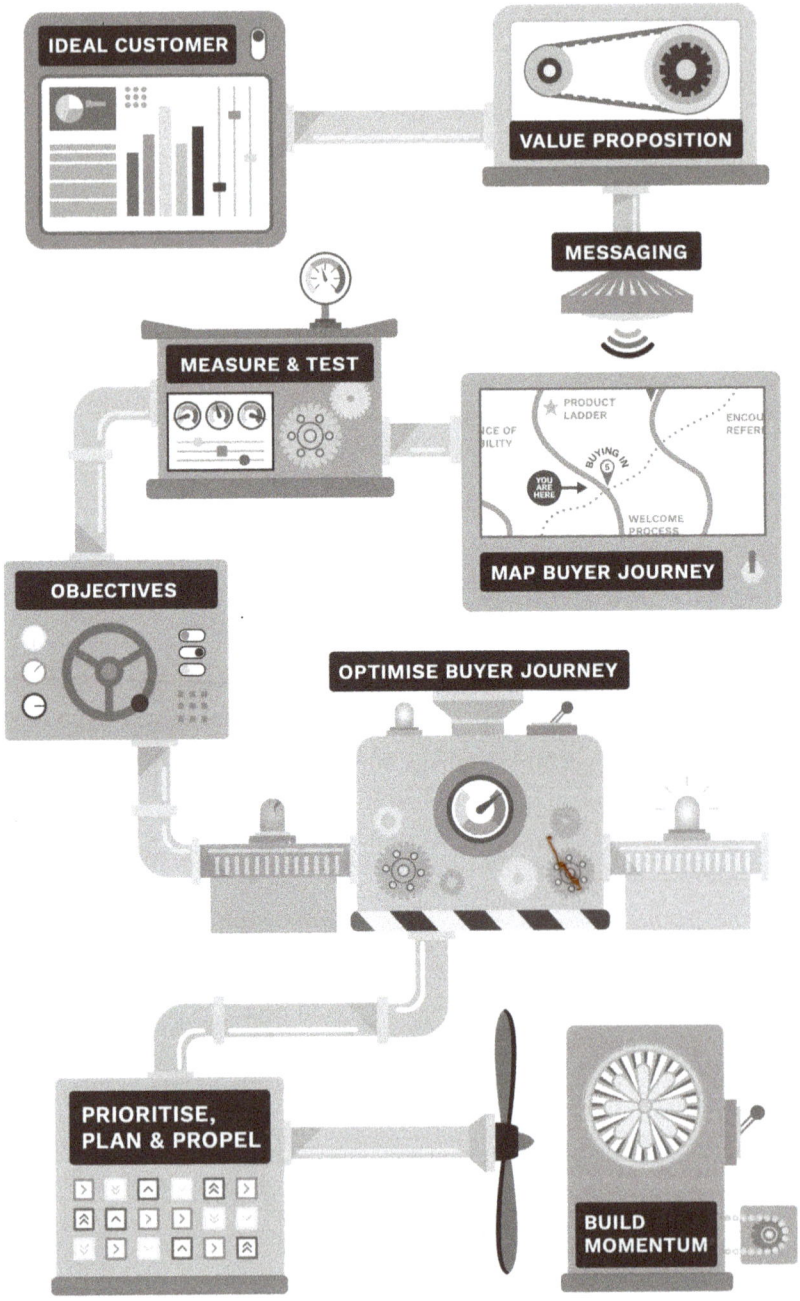

IDEAL CUSTOMER

VALUE PROPOSITION

MESSAGING

MEASURE & TEST

MAP BUYER JOURNEY

PRODUCT LADDER

BUYING IN

YOU ARE HERE

WELCOME PROCESS

OBJECTIVES

OPTIMISE BUYER JOURNEY

PRIORITISE, PLAN & PROPEL

BUILD MOMENTUM

CHAPTER 1
INTRODUCING THE MARKETING MACHINE

I used to think that marketing was complete "fluff".

I'd graduated with a degree in Mechanical Engineering and began work as a Design Engineer at a small robotics company in Bristol. We were developing bespoke, snake-like robotic arms and no one else in the world was doing what we were doing. Unfortunately that meant that no one was looking for us either.

Although our robots were amazing and world-leading, no one knew anything about them. Our prospective customers didn't understand what they were capable of, or whether these robots could solve their specific problems.

I had no experience in marketing, but I was a good communicator. One day my boss, Dr Rob Buckingham, said, "Ros, I think you'd be good in marketing and sales."

"Oh no," I thought, "I don't want to do that fluff! Marketing is all creative nonsense. I've got an engineering degree — I want to design robots!"

Rob saw something in me, and before long, I found myself working in marketing. Once I got stuck in, I realised that yes, bad marketing is fluff.

We've all seen the cringey taglines and ridiculous adverts that desperately vie for our attention and money. That's what I immediately thought of when I heard the word "marketing".

But good marketing, I learned, is methodical and structured. It's based on objective analysis and research; it's carefully designed, planned and project managed. It's measured, tested and incrementally improved; it's efficient and effective...

All of a sudden it starts to sound a lot like engineering.

And the methodology I'm going to teach you through this book has its roots in what I learned in my degree many years ago.

It's actually the same basic process that every engineer uses when they design a new product or machine:

1. Create a specification.
2. Brainstorm different ways to meet the specification.
3. Prioritise the features that are most important.
4. Design and prototype the machine.
5. Measure and test all the different components to identify which bits are working and which aren't.
6. Keep testing and improving and adding new features as needed.

If you want to design a "marketing machine" that churns out long-term loyal customers, doesn't it make sense to engineer it like this?

People manage to make marketing much more complicated than it needs to be. In truth, marketers have a vested interest in making it really complicated so that business owners have to pay them to do it. But marketing isn't a "dark art". Anyone who's intelligent enough to run a business can understand how marketing fundamentally works.

That's why I'm on a mission now: to rid the world of bad, fluff marketing!

By that, I mean marketing that's chosen without any real strategy behind it and no way of knowing whether it's going to work, or even if it *has* worked once it's been executed.

When you understand marketing, you can take control of it and you'll no longer be at the mercy of a persuasive marketer with a good sales pitch. When you take control of your marketing, any stress, doubt, and anxiety about spending money on it will begin to fade. You'll be able to focus on running your business and actually enjoy the process. You'll start to see marketing as an investment that transforms into sales and directly grows your business. You can make informed decisions using useful data from your measurements. And you can keep your marketing team and suppliers accountable, because you all know exactly what you're trying to achieve and what results you're expecting to see from your investment.

Done well, your marketing should generate long-term happy customers. If you design and build your marketing function in the same way you would design and build a machine, then your marketing will always work.

WHO IS THIS BOOK FOR?

This book is not just for engineers.

If you have a technical or scientific background, you'll definitely enjoy having a rigorous process to apply to your marketing.

Equally though, if structure and process aren't your skillset, this method will give you clarity and spark your creativity to create a better experience for your customers.

This is the book I wish I could have read 20 years ago when I first started out in marketing. A book that would cut through the nonsense and lay out, in simple terms, what marketing is all about and how you can make sure what you're doing is efficient and effective.

It's important to say that this book is specifically for small to medium-sized enterprises (SMEs), regardless of whether you're selling big-ticket services or small-ticket items. If you're a small-business owner looking for a structured, strategic and logical approach to marketing then you're in the right place.

This book is also highly relevant to charities and not-for-profit organisations because marketing is about supporting people's decision-making. If you want to encourage more people to take up your services, donate, or volunteer, then you need marketing. Throughout this book you'll just need to replace the word "customer" with "user", "donor" or "volunteer".

Over the last 20 years I've worked with hundreds of small business owners and marketing managers to move them away from what I call "gut feel" marketing and towards structured, logical marketing that they can trust and rely on.

Do you know what I mean by "gut feel" marketing? Have you ever chosen a marketing activity because it sounds like a good idea and your gut tells you it'll probably work? That's what I'm talking about.

When we don't have a structured approach to marketing then we're forced to rely on our gut. Now, don't get me wrong: if you have a marketer on your team with 10-plus years of experience then their gut feeling may well be pretty good. With 20 years of marketing experience behind me, my gut's pretty reliable! But if I only tell my clients what my gut is telling me, then they're forced to keep coming back to me for advice and that won't take away their stress and doubt. That's why I teach all my clients this structured approach — so they can control it themselves.

This book will also be valuable for marketing managers who want to make sure the work they're doing is going to translate into sales. If you're a marketing manager in an SME, this is what you'll get from this book:

1. You'll have the tools and language to clearly explain how your marketing activities are driving sales and impacting profit. This is especially helpful when you're requesting a bigger marketing budget (or even a pay rise!).

2. You'll know the right questions to ask to get the information you need from other departments in the business, such as sales and customer service or account management, so you can do your job better.

3. You'll be completely confident in what you're doing because you're working strategically and not relying on "gut feel" marketing any more.

Lastly, I also hope that marketing consultants working with small businesses will read and use the methodology in this book to do more effective marketing for their clients.

If you're a marketing consultant working with small businesses you'll be able to use the framework and methods in this book to explain exactly how your proposed marketing activities will lead to sales. This will help your clients confidently invest in the marketing activities you know will grow their businesses. I've always found it much easier to sell marketing services when I can demonstrate exactly why what I'm suggesting will lead to sales and profit.

HOW TO USE THIS BOOK

I strongly recommend you get a notebook to scribble in while you go through this book. I considered writing this book as a workbook that you'd write in, but I want you to repeat this process on a regular basis (quarterly works best for most people) and I've assumed you won't want to purchase a new copy of this book every quarter!

Please write notes in the margin of this book, highlight sections and turn the page corners down on bits you know you'll need to revisit.

This process is iterative, meaning that you will get more value from it each time you go through it. Over time, you'll learn more about your ideal customer, your strategy will evolve as your business grows, and you'll adapt your marketing activities as you discover what works really well and what doesn't.

I've created a number of resources that I use with my clients such as templates, audios, video tutorials, a journal and a reusable 90-day planner, all of which can either be downloaded or ordered via my website, rosconkie.com.

If you're going to go all-in with this, then The Marketing Machine Journal is a particularly good companion to this book. It follows the structure of this book and includes sections for everything you need to do and think about. I've been using this exact journal myself in my business for many years and I encourage all my clients to use it too (it's also available wherever you bought this book).

When you get to the buyer journey section, I also recommend using post-it notes and coloured pens (it turns out marketers really do just colour stuff in!) but I also have a digital template on my website if you're not a pen-and-paper person. You can access this, and all the resources mentioned throughout this book, at:

https://rosconkie.com/TheMarketingMachineResources

More than anything, remember this is not a theoretical textbook — I've read plenty of books on marketing theory and this is not that. This is a practical toolkit for you to use and reuse.

CHAPTER 2
WHAT IS MARKETING ANYWAY?

What do you think of when you hear the word "marketing"?

Do you think of lead generation? Getting your name out there? Generating sales? Or something else?

There are so many definitions of marketing and it seems every marketer has a slightly different one. Mine is this:

Marketing is the process of making it really easy for profitable customers to buy from you.

I like this definition because it includes all the things that can be included in the word "marketing", like distribution, customer service, packaging, pricing, and content.

The purpose of marketing is to drive sales and profit. Generating leads is one way of increasing revenue, but it's not the only way and it's by no means guaranteed that more leads will give you more sales. It also doesn't always follow that more sales means more profit.

What you really want in a business is happy, loyal customers. So think of your marketing as a "happy, loyal customer machine"!

This definition also makes it easier to understand the difference between marketing and sales. If marketing is about making it really easy for people to buy from you, then sales is about making sure people do, in fact, buy. Marketing creates the tools and resources that will support a customer through their decision-making process and Sales builds on those resources in their customer conversations to encourage them to say yes.

You may have noticed I don't use the phrase "digital marketing". In my view, this phrase is obsolete since all marketing today has a digital element to it. Even print is designed (and often printed) digitally. In my personal view the phrase "digital marketing" is akin to the word "smartphone" — you can just say "phone" because everyone will assume you're talking about a smartphone anyway. So if you find yourself talking about digital marketing (or being offered digital marketing services) you can immediately translate that into just "marketing".

In essence, the purpose of marketing is to make the role of sales much easier.

It is possible to run a business with good marketing but minimal sales, or vice versa, but you'll always be limping along. Without strong marketing and sales functions, your business will never be as profitable as it could be.

Marketing makes sales easier, while sales ensures your marketing delivers a better return on investment.

As a marketing consultant, I've met with sales teams who are sceptical of the value of marketing. My answer to them is always, "My job is to make your job really easy." Funnily enough, that always seems to get them on board!

Chances are, you are probably doing both activities but thinking of them as one or the other. And it doesn't really matter whether an activity is categorised as marketing or sales, as long as it is creating profit for your business.

So how do we make it easy for people to buy? How do we make it easy for our sales team to sell?

First, we have to understand how those profitable customers buy. Then we build trust, reduce the feeling of risk (from your customer's perspective), and deliver value at every stage of our customer's buying decision.

The outcome of good marketing is that profitable, energising customers are drawn to your business.

THE RISK OF DELEGATING YOUR MARKETING STRATEGY

Having worked for hundreds of small businesses as a consultant, I've seen how often the marketing consultancy model can put the owner of a small business in a very vulnerable position. In my view, it's really dangerous to allow your strategy to be controlled by anyone outside your business. Working with a marketing consultant is a partnership — not a chance for you to relinquish all responsibility of your strategy to an outside provider.

This is because effective marketing consultancy relies on...

1. The consultant asking all the right questions to get the information they need.
2. The consultant understanding the full context of the business and the business owner's goals and vision.
3. The consultant's skills to put all that information together and actually give really good advice.

If any of these three things don't happen, then the business owner will end up getting bad advice. This can be costly in terms of money, time and in the worst cases I've seen, damaging to the business's reputation.

It's like asking your accountant or bookkeeper to make all your financial decisions for you. They could do it... but could you ever trust someone enough to make the right decisions for your business? Could anyone outside the business understand your business well enough to know what's best?

And yet small business owners do this every day by handing over their strategy to a marketing agency or consultancy.

Now, I'm definitely not telling you to never hire a marketing consultant. I am one, and there are plenty of other good and trustworthy ones around.

However, many business owners think that if they're going to hire someone to do the implementation, then they may as well get their consultant to decide on their core strategy as well. But if you, as the business owner, don't understand the strategy your consultant has set for you, you're going to find it difficult to stop working with them if you're not happy with the results they're delivering. You'll also find it difficult to see if your marketing is actually getting you a good return on your investment.

I believe that every business owner needs and deserves to understand and control their own marketing strategy.

And, fortunately, it's not rocket science.

A marketing strategy needs to include three things:

1. Who you're specifically selling to, and what's important to them.
2. What you're selling to them, and why they'd want to buy (in particular, the problem you solve and the real value they get from your product or service).
3. How they are going to buy from you (i.e., what's the path from never having heard of you to being a loyal, raving fan).

From this, you can create a plan to improve your marketing and achieve your objectives.

If you're a relatively new business owner, strategic thinking may be a new skill for you. But don't worry — it's a skill that can be learned and improved with practice. And this book will give you all the tools you need to start.

SMALL BUSINESS MARKETING VS BIG BUSINESS MARKETING

As I've said, this book is specially designed for small business owners and this is because, in a small business, the traditional approach to marketing strategy and planning doesn't work. This is because traditional marketing approaches were designed for big businesses and just don't work when scaled down.

When I first learnt marketing theory, I was taught I must always start by doing some market research to deeply understand my current situation and market. And if you're spending millions on your marketing then yes, it makes sense to spend a small percentage of that on market research first. You can spend a few hundred grand to verify exactly what makes your audience tick and then create a strategy and plan based on that research, then roll it out across your team of marketers and agencies.

Big businesses have to do it this way because their marketing has to be consistent when it's being delivered by so many people.

But if you're a small business owner reading this book and I said to you, "Let's spend a small percentage of your marketing budget on market research," how much would that be? A few hundred quid? Maybe a couple of thousand? Let's face it — that's not going to provide much in terms of valuable market insight.

And there's another issue. If you're anything like the small-business owners I've worked with, I bet you know your customers really well. Many of my clients speak to their customers every day. They already know what's important to their customers and why they buy, so it would be a complete waste to spend their hard-earned money doing market research. The owner might not be able to articulate it all yet, but we'll come to that later in this book.

THE ALTERNATIVE: AGILE MARKETING

In engineering, there's a methodology called "Agile". Every engineer knows about it (and you may already be familiar with it too). It's all about delivering value to customers faster, with fewer problems.

Software developers found that trying to plan everything for big projects upfront didn't work, and so they came up with a better way: building software in small, manageable steps, getting feedback as they went. This approach became known as Agile Software Development because it allowed them to stay flexible and adapt as they learned. These days, the term 'Agile' gets thrown around a lot (some might say it's overused — software developers, I see you rolling your eyes!), but I'm sticking with it because it perfectly captures the iterative, step-by-step approach we're going to take to build your marketing machine.

Let me give you an example. Instead of a software company toiling away for years and then having a huge product launch, engineers will start small, delivering work regularly, and keep evaluating and improving all the time.

Now, if you're creating a huge software project that needs to be perfect the first time your customers see it (like an XBox game or something), then you have to have a comprehensive, detailed plan and then get your hundreds of developers all working to that plan. When the software is perfect, then you launch it and sell it. You have to do it that way because there are too many people involved to do anything else, and the market demands that it's perfect before you launch it.

But for most software projects, a much better approach is to create what engineers call a minimum viable product (MVP, also known as a "beta" version).

(If we're being really strict, usually a 'proof of concept' [POC] would come first, but if you're already in business and someone has bought from you, your POC is done.)

The priority now is to get people using the MVP straight away and providing feedback on what they like and dislike, then keep improving it.

The best bit about this approach is that you can have customers paying you for the product while you improve it. This is how most software is developed nowadays. If you think about software products you might use like Xero, Quickbooks, Canva or whatever CRM you use, they all use Agile. Even Microsoft and Google use Agile. It's a tried-and-trusted process.

But people don't do this in small business marketing, even though it's been proven in engineering to deliver much better results, much faster. We tend to tie ourselves in knots trying to get our marketing perfect, when it would actually be much more effective to use an Agile approach to create a marketing MVP. Then we can incrementally improve the strategy over time by testing and measuring it effectively.

Now, let me be clear: Agile does not mean creating a strategy through trial and error. An essential component of Agile is the specification, and the process starts with the minimum *viable* product.

A specification is a detailed document that includes all the requirements and functionality of the product or system that you're planning. If you give an engineer a vague specification, they may interpret it completely differently to how you envisaged, and design something totally different to what you had in mind, so it's essential to be as detailed as possible. It's no coincidence that the word 'specification' starts with 'specific'!

And a 'minimum viable product' is the most basic version of a product that meets the specification. It can be sold and then used to gather feedback from customers. It's different to a prototype because a prototype may not be in a state to sell (it may look awful and just demonstrate the functionality, or equally it may look right but doesn't actually work). A prototype gives people in the business an idea for what the product will be like, while an MVP must include the minimum level of features and design to justify selling it to customers.

To give you an example, if I was creating an accountancy software package, my prototype might be a graphical illustration of the screen where

I'd input my quotes and invoices. My MVP would actually have these features working. My MVP will have all the essential features my customers need, but it won't have any of the "nice to have" features just yet.

In the same way, your marketing must have a clear specification and a minimum viable strategy before you start.

This book is about creating that minimum viable strategy, implementing it efficiently, and testing and measuring it effectively. Once you've built your minimum viable strategy, this book will help you continue to build on it until it is a fully developed marketing machine.

A minimum viable strategy doesn't actually need to take long to make. Most small businesses can do it in less than a day — a few hours really — once you've got the hang of how to do it.

HOW "AGILE MARKETING" WORKS

To start building your Agile minimum viable strategy, you...

1. Make some assumptions.
2. Make a plan based on your assumptions.
3. Test the results to see if your assumptions were correct.
4. Adjust your plan if your original assumptions were incorrect to reflect your new assumptions.
5. Keep testing and improving.

This is a much better approach to marketing in a small business for a number of reasons. As I said before, a small business owner is typically close to their customers, so their assumptions will probably be better to begin with. The Agile approach minimises waste, creates a clear feedback loop that allows the business to keep improving its marketing processes, and works well on small budgets.

This book is about creating and implementing a structured process for marketing in your small business, and I'll give you a step-by-step system you can follow to choose marketing activities that'll make the biggest impact on your sales and profits.

You'll learn how to measure your marketing to make sure that it is efficient and effective. This transforms your marketing from a gamble into an investment that will pay off in terms of bottom-line profit. Ultimately, you'll learn how to make sure your marketing delivers sales.

WHAT TO EXPECT FROM THIS PROCESS

I don't know about you, but my social media feeds are full of ads for marketing tools and courses.

"The weird trick that business owners don't know about."

"Are you making this HUGE marketing mistake?"

"13 hacks top marketers don't want you to know about."

If you're looking for those answers, I've got bad news.

There is no weird trick that works for all businesses... except, perhaps, creating and implementing a robust strategy, which isn't weird and isn't a "trick".

There is no marketing magic wand.

A lot of clients come to me expecting me to look at their marketing and go, "Ah! Here's the ONE THING you're doing wrong. If you fix this, all your marketing problems will go away."

But it's never like that.

Invariably, the route to success in marketing is through marginal gains.

In case you're not familiar with this term, back in 2016, on the final day of the Olympic track cycling competition, Team GB Performance Director Dave Brailsford was asked for the secret to Team GB's success. He explained the "marginal gains" strategy that they had developed and implemented.

He said, "The whole principle came from the idea that if you broke down everything you could think of that goes into riding a bike, and then improved it by 1%, you will get a significant increase when you put them all together."[1] Each of these marginal gains might only add a fraction of a fraction of a millisecond, but if you add them all up it might make the difference between a medal and an "also ran".

One of the first things he taught the team was how to wash their hands (and remember, this was pre-Covid). They were all instructed to spend an extra five seconds washing their hands every time they did this, and he estimated that those five seconds per hand-wash, over the course of four years, gave them an extra five days of training by reducing infections. Those five extra days of training might only have given the team a gain of a few microseconds on the track, but at the Olympic level, those microseconds make all the difference.

The philosophy of marginal gains is undoubtedly effective, not just in cycling but in all areas of performance including in marketing, and business in general.

Success in business is usually the result of lots of small adjustments adding up over time, rather than huge seismic changes that are implemented all at once.

A marketing process is not one thing: it is a combination of many, many elements, most of which can be improved. When there are so many elements, improving each thing by a small amount adds up to a big increase in sales.

Your marketing may not be working effectively right now, but that doesn't mean you're doing it wrong. It's much more likely there are some small tweaks you can make that will start to make a big difference to the results you're getting.

---

1. Slater, M. (2012, August 8). *Olympics cycling: Marginal gains underpin Team GB dominance.* BBC News. https://www.bbc.co.uk/sport/olympics/19174302

RESOURCES

When it comes to marketing, there are two key resources we have to manage: people (or your own time, if you're a micro-business) and money.

If you want to grow your business, and don't have much in the way of finance, you'll need to put in the time and do the marketing and sales work yourself, or among your existing team. If you don't have time to do the marketing and sales yourself, you'll need to pay someone else to do it. If you have neither time nor money then you need to manage your expectations of what's realistic in terms of business growth.

Throughout the coming chapters, we're going to look at all the key components of setting and managing your marketing budget, as well as identifying exactly who needs to be on your team (and what they will be doing) to deliver the marketing results you want.

How you approach this part of the process will depend very much on where you are in your business journey.

If you're a one-person business just starting out, then you might go through this process looking at how much of your own time you can spend on your marketing and, if your cash flow allows, whether you can start to outsource a few elements of your marketing to a freelancer or virtual assistant.

If you're a more established business then you may already have a team of people and/or agencies implementing your marketing. In that case, you'll want to approach this by looking at the people and budget you have currently available and whether any of it needs changing or real-locating.

A NOTE ON MARKETING OVERWHELM

As we go through this process, you'll start thinking of lots of things you can do to improve your marketing. As your marketing wish list grows, you may start to feel overwhelmed by the prospect of implementing all these things. If that happens, keep the two following things in mind:

1. **We'll be prioritising your wish list in the chapter called Prioritise, Plan, Propel, so keep reading!** If you feel *so* overwhelmed you can't cope with any more ideas then skip forward, read about how to prioritise, and then come back to the ideas. You need to consolidate your ideas before you can prioritise them, but you may find it helpful to know exactly how you're going to manage your long wish list before you make it.

2. **Marketing is never finished.** *My* marketing is still a work in progress! I still have loads of ideas I haven't implemented yet and I think of new ideas every day. I don't worry about it, I just keep reprioritising and focusing only on my top priorities. If you have too many ideas to implement, that's great! In Prioritise, Plan, Propel, we'll prioritise the ones that'll make the biggest impact on your sales and I'll tell you to save your other ideas somewhere so you can come back to them when you've ticked off your top priorities.

CHAPTER 3
IDEAL CUSTOMER

Understanding your customer deeply is the foundation of your marketing strategy.

If we're designing a machine that will churn out long-term, loyal customers, then it's paramount we're clear on exactly who we want this machine to produce. Your ideal customer is essentially the raw material we're putting into our machine, so we need to know as much about them as possible.

One of the first questions I ask all my clients is, "Who is your ideal customer?"

It sounds like it should be quite an easy question to answer, doesn't it?

However, when I ask this question, the answer I most often hear is... "Anyone!"

Sometimes I hear, "Women." Sometimes it's more specific: "Women aged 25-60."

Another one I often hear is "All small business owners."

Well, according to the Department for Business and Trade at the time of going to print, there were about 5.5 million SMEs in the UK.[1]

Is that specific enough?

Surely a customer is a customer? Yes and no.

Not all customers are created equal. Some customers take a lot of nurturing to get over the line, then they only buy once and complain because this wasn't really what they wanted or needed.

I know you don't want to spend your time and money attracting THOSE kinds of customers!

I'm sure I don't need to tell you that the most profitable businesses are the ones with lots of highly profitable customers. But a lot of people forget this. You want your marketing to produce long-term, loyal customers. Profitable customers. Customers who rave about you to their friends and colleagues and who write glowing reviews about you.

If you've created an ideal customer persona before but struggled to see the value in it, don't worry. Most marketers start by asking you to draw your ideal customer, give them a name and then fill in lots of demographic information, like how old they are, where they live, their gender, and what books they read.

The thing is, if your business is like mine (and most of my clients), then a lot of this information is irrelevant.

When I was trying to market multi-million pound robots, it made absolutely no difference whether the buyer was a 38-year-old man from Cumbria who read John Grisham, or a 59-year-old woman from Geneva who loved Agatha Christie.

What mattered was they...

---

1.   Department for Business & Trade. (2024, October 3). *Business population estimates for the UK and regions 2024: statistical release.* https://www.gov.uk/government/statistics/business-population-estimates-2024/business-population-estimates-for-the-uk-and-regions-2024-statistical-release

- Needed our product.
- Had the budget to spend on our product.
- Were profitable for our business.
- Were energising to work with.
- Would get the full benefit of everything we had to offer.

People who tick all these boxes are much more likely to buy from you.

If a customer doesn't get value for money from what you deliver then...

1. They won't buy more than once.
2. They won't give you a testimonial or refer you to their friends/associates.
3. They'll probably not be very enjoyable to work with.

So what does an amazing customer look like for your business?

Imagine someone who'd be a perfect match for your business: how easy would it be to sell your products or services to them? It'd be easy, of course! They desperately need to fix the problem you solve, they have the budget and they'll get loads of value from what you offer.

The closer someone is to being your ideal customer, the easier it will be to sell to them. Niching down isn't about limiting your business — it's about becoming the obvious choice for the clients you want most.

At the same time, people who are less like your ideal customer will be harder to sell to. The sale will take more effort and more resources. You might still sell something to them, but it's less likely. It'll be a tougher sell because they won't be getting as much value for their money, and they may not be as profitable for you because they may not buy as much from you over the long-term.

If we're investing money in attracting people to your business, we want to make sure that investment gives you the biggest return possible. So, we want to focus your marketing spend on people who'll be most likely to buy from you. Later in this book we'll go into detail about how to make sure you're attracting your ideal customer, but to do that we first need to be completely clear and specific about who that person is.

Looking at this another way, if you've got, say, £100 to spend on a marketing activity, would you spend it specifically on attracting people who are close to being your ideal customer (targeted marketing)? Or would you spread your budget across a wide audience that includes a load of people who will probably never buy from you ("scattergun" marketing)?

If you aim your marketing at everyone, then you'll have to spread your budget thinly. Alternatively, if you concentrate your budget on promoting only to people who are much more likely to buy from you, you'll get a more efficient result and a better return on your investment (ROI).

We'll cover what this looks like in practice later in this book but, to give you an example, it's the difference between putting an advert on the back of a bus (scattergun, since everyone will see it) and putting an advert in a niche industry magazine that only your audience reads (targeted). This is because when something is irrelevant to us then we immediately ignore it (or hit 'delete') — which means that the cost of showing us that marketing message is wasted. You may have to be more creative in how you get targeted marketing in front of people, but you'll get a much better result in terms of ROI.

More than that, if you tighten your focus specifically to one ideal customer persona, or avatar, the following things will happen:

1. You'll clearly understand the problems they face and that you solve.
2. You'll be able to figure out what you need to say about your product and how you need to say it.
3. It'll be easier to decide what to include in your product or service and what to leave out because you'll know what is most valuable to your audience.
4. When you start planning your promotional activities, you'll know where to spend your money and where not to bother.

However specific you think you're being, when defining your ideal customer, you probably need to be more specific.

There's an aphorism I love which is: "Time spent in reconnaissance is never wasted."

The time you spend working on this strategic stuff will pay dividends to your business.

And the interesting thing is that every business has a different ideal customer. Even if your business is similar to a competitor, you won't be exactly the same as them. You can't be, because you are different people with different personalities and values, and your businesses (and customers) will reflect that.

This is why 'copy and paste' marketing doesn't work. I often hear, "This seems to work really well for our competitors so we think we should do it."[2] But if you have a different ideal customer to your competitors then it may not work as effectively for you. It might, but people waste a lot of money doing this kind of "trial and error" marketing.

CREATING YOUR IDEAL CUSTOMER PERSONA

In a moment I'm going to share the checklist I use with my clients when creating an ideal customer persona. I've refined it over many years of working with clients in all sorts of industries; from aerospace suppliers, engineering consultancies, manufacturers and software developers, to virtual assistants, therapists, coaches and graphic designers.

If you are already working with a dream customer (someone you wish you could clone), picture them. If not, try to imagine the person that you would climb over everybody else to speak to if they walked into the room at an event. Sometimes an ideal customer is a mixture of a number of really good customers you know well. Sometimes it's a completely made-up person. The important thing is that they're real in your mind. You need a vivid persona for this.

---

2. How do you know it's effective for your competitors? How much money are they spending on it and how much is it delivering in sales? Unless you have this data you can't know for sure if it's delivering ROI for them. They could be doing some other marketing activities you're not aware of that are delivering the success you're seeing.

If you're picturing a dream customer who already knows you well, for this exercise you need to imagine a clone of them who's never heard of you before. We're going to look at attitudes and questions, so we need to imagine someone who knows nothing about you, and who doesn't know if you're any good.

If you sell to a few different types of people (or markets), pick one for this exercise. Once you've been through the checklist for one market you can go back and do the process again for other markets, but it's too confusing to try and do it for more than one ideal customer at a time.

For small businesses with several ideal customer personas, it's often beneficial to focus on one ideal customer for 90 days. Work on improving your marketing for that audience for 90 days, and then choose a different persona in three months' time. Of course, you're not going to stop marketing and selling to the other audiences, you're just focusing your attention on improving your marketing to one audience at a time. This makes the strategy and planning process much easier to manage, since you only need to think about one ideal customer, one proposition, and one buyer journey. The more strategies you have to hold in your head, the easier it is to get confused and overwhelmed.

If you sell to businesses, remember that a business doesn't make a decision — a human being does. Marketing is all about helping people make decisions, so who is the person who has to make a decision? You may have a few people involved in the decision-making process, in which case it's worth going through this process for each person separately. To begin with, pick the most important or most influential decision-maker.

If you find you're really struggling with this part of the process, move on to the next chapter, Value Proposition, and then come back to this afterwards. It doesn't matter whether you do your Ideal Customer Persona or Value Proposition first, as long as you have defined both by the time you move on to the next step.

Now put this book down for a couple of minutes to get a really clear idea of that person in your mind, then come back to read through the next steps.

I recommend my clients give their ideal customer a name. This helps them stay focused on the customer and also helps their team communications, so everyone knows which market they're talking about ("What would 'Sarah' think of this new feature?").

Have you got a really clear picture of your ideal customer in your mind?

Now get out of your own head and into your ideal customer's mind. They've never bought from you before and they don't know anything about your business.

Start a new page in your notebook, or turn to the "Customer Persona" page in your Marketing Machine Journal, and write down as much as you can think of for each of the following questions.

You may find it helpful to work with a partner or colleague on this. Get them to ask you the questions from the checklist below and answer them out loud while they write down your answers for you. Or get an AI tool to transcribe your conversation for you.

ATTITUDES

- What is their attitude to your industry, niche and/or particular area of expertise? When they hear of your industry, what do they think of?
- What is their attitude to your product/service?
- What is their attitude to the alternatives to your product or service?
- What do they love about what you do/your industry?
- What do they dislike or resent about what you do/your industry?
- What do they believe about your industry, and about your product or service? Are there any pervasive myths about your industry or category?
- What are their values — what's important to them?

Identifying your ideal customer's attitudes and beliefs about your industry is really important because it means you can create marketing messages that will resonate with them. You'll be able to show your customers you understand them and can empathise with them.

Here's an example of one of our ideal customers: the CEO of an engineering consultancy.

> If you ask any of his friends what he does they'll tell you he's in tech or "an engineer," but they can't tell you in any more detail because none of them understand what he does.
>
> He's very process-driven, systems-oriented and loves a good spreadsheet... but no one in his business really understands marketing. They all think it's "creative nonsense" which isn't relevant to their business. They tried posting on social media for a while, and tried Google Ads and a few other marketing "things" but it was expensive and they didn't see any impact from any of it.
>
> Currently all their business comes from word of mouth and the occasional exhibition, but they want to grow and these two channels won't generate the sales they need. Plus they have no control over when the referrals come in. They don't know how to get from where they are to where they want to be, and the pressure of increasing sales is stressful and frustrating.
>
> He feels exasperated when customers go to competitors as he knows that they're making the wrong decision, and he doesn't understand why his customers don't see why his offering is so much better.

These traits make him a great client for us because we can help him articulate exactly what he does in plain English and why it's important to his customers. We can help him understand the fundamentals of how marketing works and teach him how to use his process-oriented approach to benefit his marketing.

Go into as much depth as you can here. Really articulate everything you can think of that's going on for them. The better you understand your customer, the better your marketing will be. If you'd like to see a fully worked-up example of an ideal customer persona, so you can see the level of detail I'm talking about, you can download our ideal customer persona example from my website.[3]

QUESTIONS, CONCERNS AND OBJECTIONS

- What is the impact of a bad decision for this customer? Remember, they don't know anything about your business right now because they've never bought from you before. What would happen if they choose your product or service and you turn out to be no good? What won't happen? What are the implications?
- Who else will be impacted if they make a bad buying decision? Will it affect their family, their colleagues, or their boss? Who else? And what would this knock-on effect mean for your ideal customer?
- What concerns might they have about buying? It doesn't matter whether you think these concerns are valid or not — if the customer may have these concerns, we need to consider them and address them in our marketing.
- What questions do they have? Think about what questions you're often asked by customers. And what questions or concerns might they think but not ask out loud?
- What do they believe about you or your industry that isn't true? Are there any myths about your industry that your ideal customer might believe?
- What reasons might they give to avoid making this decision?
- What reasons might they give for buying an alternative instead of choosing you?

---

3. https://rosconkie.com/TheMarketingMachineResources

By answering these questions in as much depth as you can, you'll identify all the objections and concerns buyers might raise when buying from you. Your marketing needs to overcome as many of them as possible if your customer is going to feel confident they're making the right choice. Objections and questions make great topics for content like blogs, infographics and videos. If you've identified some key objections then it may be useful to put them on an Frequently Asked Questions (FAQ) page on your website or turn them into "The Ultimate Guide to [what you do]".

Going back to my earlier example, some of my ideal customer's questions and concerns include:

- "I've worked with marketers in the past but haven't seen any results from it.
- Is marketing support worth the money when AI could write my strategy, plan and content for me?"
- "How am I going to know if this is working?"
- "How long will it take to see results?"
- "How much of my time will this take up?"
- "How much is this going to cost?"
- "Is marketing actually my top priority or are there other things that are more important at the moment?"
- "How are you going to get my team on board too? They're all engineers and not sure about this marketing thing."

THEIR BUYING HABITS

- How often do they buy what you offer?
- How often do they think about what you offer/your industry?
- How long does it take them, typically, to choose a product such as yours? (Consider the maximum and minimum time to a decision, if it varies a lot)
- How much time are they likely to spend thinking about the decision during this timeframe? (e.g. they might spend almost

a day over the course of a week, or a couple of hours over the course of six months.)

For some buying decisions, people make their decision quite quickly, say in a day, but on that day they might spend a few hours considering the decision. Other decisions might be made over the course of several weeks or even months, but over that time the buyer doesn't actually spend much time thinking about the decision. Some decisions take an hour and the whole hour is spent on that decision.

Think about these two different timescales for your buyer: the timespan of the buying journey (from 'never heard of you' to 'buying from you') and the time your buyer spends in active consideration.

These timescales are useful to understand because, if your buyer typically spends a couple of hours in active consideration before they're comfortable buying, then your marketing needs to enable people to spend that much time with you. This is where content like blogs, videos, and podcasts come in because they allow people to "spend time with you" before they buy.

In my business, our ideal customer often takes four to eight months to make a decision. However, once they decide to go ahead, they often want to get started straight away. It often won't be their first time investing in their marketing, but many have had their fingers burned in the past.

THEIR INFLUENCERS

- What is your buyer's role in the decision-making process? For example, are they the budget-holder? Do they have to recommend a solution to their boss or other budget-holder? Will they use the product or service themselves or are they buying for someone else to use?
- Who will influence them during this buying decision? Will they ask someone's advice when they're considering buying? Do they make their buying decision in isolation or is there

someone else who could veto the decision, like a partner, boss or family member? Who else might influence their decision?

If your buyer has some critical influencers or people who could veto the decision then it can be useful to consider those people's attitudes and objections as well. In some cases I recommend treating key influencers as customers themselves, since they also have to go through a decision-making process and have to buy into the product or service.

You have to support the influencer's decision too and they may well have different objections to your buyer. For example, they may be much more interested in the cost, or the logistics of delivery, or the time it will take, than your buyer. If they have different objections to your customer then your marketing needs to answer those concerns too.

In doing this exercise, you might discover that there are key types of people or places where your buyer is likely to go for recommendations. For example, I'm often recommended to business owners by other trusted advisors, such as accountants, business coaches and sales trainers. I make sure I build good relationships with these people so they remember to mention my name when they're asked the question, "I need some help with my marketing strategy, do you know anyone good?"

Your ideal customer might have a favourite podcast that's relevant to what you do, so you may want to find out how to become a guest on the show. Or they might use a particular industry directory or resource to look for suppliers, in which case this will be important to consider when we start looking at how we can improve your marketing.

Your message needs to be in front of those people and in those places so your name comes up when people ask for a recommendation. I'll explain how to apply all this later in the book. For now, just get all your ideas down on paper. Highlight the key influencers now so you can refer back to them later.

RED FLAGS

Have you ever had a customer who takes so much of your energy you wished you'd never agreed to work with them in the first place? Unfortunately, I have. And, if I'm honest, there were warning signs early on that would've saved me a lot of time and hassle if I'd paid more attention to them.

This doesn't apply to all businesses, so feel free to disregard this section if it's not relevant to you. However, it can often be useful to consider what makes a bad customer — someone who takes a lot of resources to service and drains you and your employees of energy. Here are the questions to ask that will help you identify these potential customers:

- What were the warning signals you've ignored in the past that were telling you a customer was going to turn out to be difficult or de-energising for you?
- What might someone say, do or think that will indicate they're not going to be a good customer for you?
- What attitudes or beliefs indicate someone will not be a good customer for you?

For me, a red flag is, "I know what I need to do, I just don't have the time to do it." If someone has a marketing shopping list they just want someone to execute, then I'm not the right person to help them — I don't want to execute any marketing activities unless I'm confident in the strategy behind them.

For one of my clients, a graphic design agency, a red flag is asking how much something will cost before they've discussed what they actually need. "How much is a logo?" is a red flag that indicates the customer is primarily interested in getting something cheap, and less interested in having a quality brand. They listen out for it and, with the help of a couple of carefully planned follow-up questions, can now avoid investing time and energy in a prospect who's highly unlikely to become a good client.

DEMOGRAPHIC AND PERSONAL PREFERENCES

So many marketers start with this. When I was first taught how to create an ideal customer persona, demographic information was all I was told to include. But if you start here, it's so easy to get bogged down in irrelevant information that distracts you from the things that are really important to your customer.

So, lastly, and only if you can do this without stereotyping, consider your ideal customer's demographic and preferences.

There's tonnes of stuff people include here but, as I said, it's not always relevant so only include what's actually important.

Go through the list below and just ignore anything that isn't relevant.

For example, for us it's important I'm working with the business owner or CEO. But it doesn't matter what their age, gender, location, education level etc. is, so I leave all that out. It might matter for your business, so here is a list of demographic details you can collect:

- Age, gender, occupation and/or job title
- Location
- Income and level of education
- Marital status/number and age of children
- Social media they use
- Newspapers/books/magazines they read
- Websites they visit and blogs they read
- Thought leaders they look up to
- Causes or charities they support
- Issues they are concerned about

If in doubt, leave it out. You can always add it in later if you realise it's relevant.

It's quite common to find this ideal customer persona process quite difficult, especially the first few times you do it. Putting yourself in your customer's shoes is a skill that can take a bit of time and practice to build. If you're really struggling, schedule 30 minutes or so in your diary every few weeks or once a month to repeat this exercise and build this skill.

DRAWING OUT CONTENT IDEAS FROM YOUR IDEAL CUSTOMER PERSONA

Now you've created your ideal customer persona, it's worthwhile going back over it to glean content ideas. Open a new page in your notebook or turn to the Content and Messaging Ideas page in your Marketing Machine Journal and write down all your ideas for content so you can refer back to them when it's time to start creating.

First, look back through the questions, concerns and objections you wrote down. Are they worried about the cost? Unsure whether your solution will fit their needs? Concerned about switching from their current provider? Use these concerns to generate content that addresses these issues head-on, reassuring them and reducing friction in the decision-making process.

If a customer asked you this question, how would you answer it? Any question where the answer is "it depends" needs to be a piece of content that explains what "it" depends on, and educates your customer to make an informed buying decision. Think of ways you'd explain things and how a customer could ask the question in different ways.

For example, 'The 7 key criteria that affect the cost of an engineering design project' or 'Everything you need to know before switching to a new IT services provider'.

Also look out for case studies you've written (or could write) that address these concerns.

What do you find yourself saying or explaining to customers on a regular basis? Are there any analogies or stories you find yourself repeating often? If you find yourself using them a lot in conversations with customers then chances are they'd make a great piece of content.

Look at the attitude of your customer to your industry. If they see your product or service as a "necessary evil", what would you say to them to change their mind? Or perhaps they're right to think that and what they need is tips to solve the problem as quickly and painlessly as possible?

For example, '6 ways to save money on bespoke software' or 'The top 5 signs it's time to upgrade your service desk system.'

What would you want to hear if you were in their situation? Are there any similarities between your experience and that of your customers? What would you advise a friend if they were in your customer's situation (and you were not in a position to sell to them for some reason)? What advice would you give them? For example, '10 questions to ask your marketing consultant before you hire them.'

By using your customer persona to guide your content creation, you'll ensure every piece of content you produce is relevant, targeted, and speaks directly to the needs of your ideal customer. And when you do that, you'll build trust and demonstrate you are a trustworthy authority in your industry.

———

END OF CHAPTER CHECKLIST

I have:

☐ Identified who my ideal customer persona is.

☐ Articulated their attitudes to my industry, category or business.

☐ Written down their questions, concerns and objections.

☐ Identified any red flags to watch out for.

☐ Completed my persona with their buying habits and demographic information.

☐ Identified ideas for content I could create and added them to my Content and Messaging Ideas list.

CHAPTER 4
VALUE PROPOSITION

Why do people buy anything?

There are only two reasons that people buy:

1. To solve or get away from a problem.
2. To move towards something they desire.

Most businesses deliver both, but the proportions differ. Some businesses deliver products and services that are heavily weighted towards solving problems with only a small 'desire' element. Others are more desire-satisfying. Some products are 100% desire-satisfying: from jewellery to ice cream, I'm sure you can think of many in this category. A small number are 100% problem-solving, from postage stamps to washing-up liquid — just think of the last time you sighed and thought, "Yes, I suppose I need that."

If you're thinking that your product or service is 100% problem-solving then I'd encourage you to look again and really think about the emotional reasons why someone might buy from you. It's easy to think that, for example, bottled water is a 100% problem-solving product. Evian, Fiji and other premium brands would beg to differ. Selling a product on problem-solving alone is difficult because it is the emotional part of our brain that triggers desire and prompts us to take action.

In this chapter we're going to look at both "problem" and "desire". Keep an open mind: you may be surprised to find that your product or service doesn't have the balance you expect.

Now, I want you to start thinking about the transfer of value between you and your customer.

You give your customer value in terms of your product or service, your advice and your support.

Your customer gives you value in terms of their money, their data, a testimonial or case study, and the recommendations they make to their friends.

This exchange of value is important to understand because people will not give you value (usually money) if they don't see the value they'll get in return. It's crucial that your business effectively communicates this value so your customers can buy confidently.

Marketers often say that a customer's most common question is: "What's in it for me?" If you don't answer this question through your marketing, then your customer has to work it out for themselves. This may not seem like a lot of effort to you since you *know* the value you deliver, but we want to make it as easy as possible for people to buy. If your customers have to join the dots themselves, that's not making it easy for them to buy.

If you regularly get objections about the price of your product or service then chances are you're not communicating the true value well enough. It's never about the money: people will spend vast amounts of money on things they really value (such as a house, a car, a famous artwork etc), so when someone says "It's a bit expensive," what they're really saying is, "I'm not seeing enough value."

If you can explain the true value your customers are going to get, their response to seeing the price will change to, "Wow that's really good value, sign me up!"

WHAT IS A VALUE PROPOSITION?

Your value proposition describes the real value you deliver to your customers. It's not about what you sell, but why it's important. A value proposition isn't the same as a slogan, and it's not a soundbite to be used on your website. Instead it's an internal tool you'll use to inform your messaging. It's also something you'll use to brief your marketing team and suppliers so they are all aligned with your strategy.

A lot of marketers recommend people distil their value proposition into a paragraph, often using a templated structure such as "We help [audience] to do/have [benefits] by doing [solution]". The problem with this is that by condensing your value proposition down, you end up removing the richness that makes it valuable to you as a business. A one-line value proposition statement is about as useful as saying my ideal customer persona is "small business owners" — not very useful at all.

So I'm going to show you how to create a thorough value proposition that you'll be able to use to inform the messaging you use in your marketing.

Some marketers start by creating a value proposition and then create a customer persona to match it. It's not wrong to do it that way because your goal is to have a proposition and customer persona that fit together perfectly, like two pieces of a jigsaw.

Start-ups and companies with brand new products may want to outline a proposition first, then go out to their audience to refine their customer persona, then come back to the proposition to make sure they fit each together neatly.

There can sometimes be a bit of back-and-forth between ideal customer and value proposition in the early stages of a strategy, especially if your business is relatively new, or if you haven't done much strategic work before.

I like to start with the customer persona — most businesses have a fairly good idea of what they deliver, but far too few have real clarity on their ideal customer. Both pieces of the jigsaw need to be well-defined, so it's best to start with the less defined piece. We tackled the ideal customer in the last chapter, but you might find that, by going through the exercises in this chapter, you will gain more clarity on your ideal customer as well as your value proposition.

Find a new page in your journal, and grab your brainstorming buddy again if that would be helpful. Work through these value proposition questions and then set aside some time to go back to your ideal customer notes afterwards to add in anything that has come up.

"AWAY FROM"

What *specifically* is the problem you solve for your ideal customer?

Imagine yourself in your ideal customer's shoes again: what is their situation before they encounter your business?

What are they struggling with?

What are they annoyed about?

What do they find frustrating or stressful?

Paint a picture of the doom and gloom of life before they meet you.

Another question marketers love to ask is, "Where's the pain?" and the doom and gloom is what they're talking about. Whether you sell software, accountancy, personal training or engineering consultancy, you solve a problem for your customer. It's worth spending time thinking about this because it'll make your marketing messages so much more powerful.

Look for the problems.

Once you've identified the problem (or problems) you solve, ask yourself, "Why is it important to my customer that this problem is solved?"

What will happen if it is not solved? What *won't* happen if it *is* solved?

What is the real impact of this problem on your customer?

If you're sure that your business is 100% desire-driven, think about your ideal customer's situation before they buy from you and identify the emotional pain that your product or service resolves. And, again, ask yourself, "Why is it important to my customer that this is resolved?"

Dig deep here. It's often useful to do this exercise with someone who can act like a toddler repeatedly asking, "Why is that?" until you get right to the heart of the problem.

To give you an example, an engineering consultancy might identify that their clients don't have the time or skills to implement a project that would reduce the risk of on-site accidents occurring. So now we need to ask ourselves, "What will happen if this isn't solved?" The potential result of this problem not being solved would be an incident on-site. Health & Safety would investigate and discover it was preventable. Hefty fines would follow, plus a whole lot of wasted time and stress. The worst case scenario is that someone dies and the CEO has to live with their guilt for the rest of their life... and they're sacked, obviously.

All of a sudden, a problem which initially looked relatively mundane (not having the time or skills) suddenly looks a whole lot more important and is much more likely to be prioritised. And can you spot all the emotions we've identified? Fear, stress, guilt, anxiety... these are really important to consider in your marketing, because those are the things people will take action to get away from.

Of course, "You could DIE if you don't act NOW!!" is probably not an appropriate headline for your website. We all have that very useful safety mechanism in our brain that I like to call the, "That will never happen to me" switch. But it's important to help our prospects fully weigh up their decisions — without sensationalism — so that they can make informed choices.

Your product may not have such a dramatic "away from" effect. It could be things like:

- The stress of juggling too many tasks.
- The anxiety of not knowing what to do next.
- The stress of not having enough time or money.

- The fear of something bad happening.
- The anxiety of having to keep up with changing technology, family needs or industry regulations.

I used to think that people came to me because they wanted a marketing plan, because that's what they all asked for. But not having a marketing plan isn't actually the problem. In reality, no one wants a marketing plan! What they really want is...

- To stop wasting time and money on marketing that doesn't deliver results.
- To stop wasting time overthinking what they should do.
- To see their business growing to its full potential.
- To stop feeling the stress and doubt that they're currently feeling about whether their marketing is working.

And many other reasons.

People might come to you for *what* you do, but your value proposition needs to explain *why* they want what you're selling.

There are a million examples of "away from" emotions I could list, so go back to your ideal customer's situation and dig into how they feel. What are they trying to get away from, and what are the specific emotions they want to stop feeling about their problem? Write it all down in your notebook, journal or strategy document.

If we focus all our marketing messaging on the face-value problem (such as "We provide specialist skills" or "We save you time") then we're forcing our customers to do the hard work of thinking about the implications of these things (i.e. the emotions triggered by these problems). Your customers are busy people and, chances are, they don't want to spend any unnecessary time on this decision. We need to help them think it through and show them the implications of their choices. Then it's up to them if they want to try it.

The other important factor is that if your customer sees this as a trivial or mundane problem, they're less likely to want to pay a lot of money to fix it. If you can show them how significant this problem really is, and that the solution you're offering will rescue them from an even bigger problem, they're more likely to see the value they'll get in exchange for their money.

SPARKS

A few years ago our house was burgled. My husband had occasionally raised the question previously of whether we should get a security system, and I always said, "We live in a safe area, is it really worth the hassle and expense?"

My "That'll never happen to me" switch was in full effect.

After the break-in, my husband and I both spent the evening diligently researching home security systems. We bought an expensive system and installed it as quickly as we possibly could.

In the space of a day, we went from thinking we probably didn't need a security system to feeling that buying one was the single most important thing for us to do at that moment.

I call these moments "sparks".

In this case, it was a quick, fairly dramatic experience that sparked us to realise we needed a solution to this problem.

Often sparks are less dramatic. A conversation prompts your customer to realise they need help with something. A missed opportunity causes them to decide they need to make a change. A seemingly insignificant moment becomes the last straw that provokes a flurry of action.

Some problems appear suddenly and feel acute, like a burglary. Others are slow-building and chronic — you don't notice you're suffering until something happens that makes you decide that you can't go on like this.

Another spark moment I had was triggered by a niggling back pain that was gradually getting worse. It was annoying but I just put up with it because it wasn't interfering too much with my life. But when my husband told me that I had to get used to things like this because I was "getting old", I instantly resolved to find a solution. I wasn't even 40 at the time! There was no way I was going to accept that I was just getting old, so it had to be fixed. Fortunately I already knew a chiropractor, and I spent that evening researching and texting friends asking for extra recommendations.

Go back to your ideal customer's situation before they meet you. What type of occurrence or interaction would spark them to think, "I need to fix this, right now"?

What might they see, or hear, or feel to make them decide they're not going to tolerate the problem anymore?

Write it all down.

I love sparks because they're like mini-stories. Human beings love stories, and we're much more likely to remember a story than facts and information, especially if it's a story that resonates with us. And that's how we'll use these sparks: as mini-stories for our content (more on content later, but it could be anything from blog posts and social media updates to videos, podcasts and ebooks).

A burglar alarm company could write a really useful blog called '5 things to do if you've been burgled.' Only one of the recommendations might be to get a burglar alarm. Another piece of content might be, '10 things to consider before buying a burglar alarm' or 'What level of security does your home need? A breakdown of the different types and when to choose them.'

The chiropractor could make a video on the subject of the changes to expect in your joints as you age, and the changes that are preventable.

I could go on. Go through what you've written so far and make a note of any content ideas so you can use them later.

"TOWARDS"

You've looked at the "away from" emotions that your customers are feeling before they buy from you, and you've identified the sparks that might trigger someone to realise they need to change. Now we're looking at how your customers feel *after* working with you. What is the light at the end of the tunnel that you are leading them towards?

Sit back for a moment and think about the *real* value people get when they buy your product or service.

What have they gained after buying from you?

How do they feel after they've received this value?

Why is this important? What is the impact on their life?

What is it they really *want*? What is the desire you are satisfying?

In some businesses, customers get value immediately when they purchase. For others, it can take time to get value. For example, visiting the chiropractor delivered immediate relief from the pain I had been experiencing, but it took a while for my home alarm system to get set up and start delivering value. When I deliver training to clients, they immediately feel reassured that they're taking steps in the right direction. Soon they'll feel more confident about their marketing and that it's going to work, but the ultimate benefits often take a while — they might not see results on their bottom line for months afterwards.

Write down what people might have and feel straight away (or soon after buying), and then also write down the ultimate benefits that people will get once they've got the full value of what you offer.

If you find this difficult, it can help to look back at testimonials and reviews: what have your customers said about the value they've got from working with you? Think about specific people you've worked with and how they feel now, having got the full value of what you offer.

Again, be the persistent toddler and ask why that is important to them until you really get down to the core of it.

What do these benefits give your customers?

And what does that mean for them?

The light at the end of the tunnel for a customer-focused accountancy firm might be that customers are fully aware of their liability every month. This means they have visibility of their company profits and costs, so they can plan ahead for their tax bill, and know when and how much they can invest in different areas of the business. They feel protected, safe and supported.

I worked with a client, True Position Robotics (TPR), who makes very specific, highly accurate robotic drilling systems for the aerospace industry. Whenever we asked them about what value their customers got from these systems, they'd talk more about how accurate their robot drilling systems were. I kept asking, "Why is that important to your customers? Why do they need systems to be that accurate? What does this level of accuracy give them?" (I can be the annoying toddler too.) Eventually we got to the crux of it: it helps their customers reduce their carbon footprint. TPR's robots are smaller and lighter than other options on the market, so they use less electricity and the accuracy prevents mistakes. This reduces waste, which means less carbon in the customer's footprint.

As I write, the aerospace industry is under intense pressure from both customers and governments to reduce carbon emissions due to the industry's impact on global climate change. In just a few years, Net Zero has become an existential question for every aerospace player. For TPR, this is the key to their value proposition. If these companies can't make significant changes, then they'll likely face increased regulation and spiralling costs as well as losing market share if their competitors are more successful in cutting their carbon footprint. So now, instead of talking about accurate drilling, the business owner leads with how TPR's systems can get their customers closer to Net Zero. You can imagine how this really makes people sit up and listen!

Not only are these "towards" messages useful in your marketing, they're also useful to remind your staff of the real purpose of the company and the impact their jobs are making to customers' lives. A lot of people find it very motivating to see how their small role results in significant and positive outcomes for the people they're serving. It can also positively impact company culture and customer service to talk internally about these outcomes.

YOU DON'T NEED A USP!

I need to say at this point that you don't need a "Unique Selling Proposition". This is a big marketing bugbear of mine because so many marketers insist you need a USP.

In case you've never heard the phrase, a USP is a distinctive feature or benefit that sets you apart from your competitors.

The reason I hate the phrase is because of the word "unique": it forces people to look outward to similar businesses and scrutinise how exactly they are different. The differences between you and another business in your industry may be impossible to describe. You might know that you're more customer-focused than most of your competitors, but that's very subjective and hardly unique, is it? And if it's not unique does that mean it's not worth talking about?

Essentially, every business is inherently unique in the same way that every human being is unique. Maybe the key difference between your business and a competitor's is simply down to the differences in personality between you and the other owner. Yet I've seen so many people tie themselves in knots trying to find a USP and getting completely stuck because other people also do what they are doing.

Instead, think about what you're particularly good at. What are your strengths? What are you known for in the industry? Why do your customers say they keep coming back to work with you?

The best way to differentiate your business from others in your industry is to show it — not to tell it. Working in engineering in the early 2000s, almost every business I encountered had the word "innovative" on the homepage of their website. Often multiple times. Everyone thinks they're innovative; not everyone actually is. Customer service is another area that most businesses claim to prioritise; not all of them actually do. So don't say, "We're different because we have great customer service." *Show* you have great customer service — demonstrate your differences through your behaviour and the way you do business. You do this with content: help people get to know you by sharing articles and videos that highlight your values and your knowledge. People will believe that customer service is important to you if you are helpful and generous *before* they become a customer.

Write down what's important to you in the context of your work. Your values and what's important to you set the tone for your marketing and how you describe what you do and why people buy.

ALTERNATIVES

Most marketers usually call this bit "competitor analysis", but I find the word "competitor" unhelpful, because most people immediately think of other businesses that do the same thing as them. However, working with a competitor is not your ideal customer's only option.

Your customers have choices. They could buy what you offer, or they could do something else entirely. What else might they choose to do?

In my first graduate job at the niche robotics company, we had literally zero competitors. No one in the whole world was doing what we were doing (and we spent a long time looking!).

We might not have had competitors, but we did have "alternatives".

For the robotics company, the alternatives were things like...

- Using other, more well-known technologies.
- Using other types of robot.
- Deciding it's too costly to fix the problem and so do nothing.

For me as a marketing consultant, the alternatives for my customers include...

- Carrying on as they are.
- Hiring a marketing apprentice or marketing assistant and hoping they can do all the marketing.
- Hiring an agency that promises overnight results.
- Asking an AI to build their marketing strategy and create all the content.

A lot of my clients come to me after discovering that none of these options worked very well for them.

So what might your customer do instead of buying from you? Make a list.

Once you have your list, sit with each option and ask yourself, in what situation(s) would this actually be a good choice?

What are the advantages of this option over buying from us?

Doing nothing is much cheaper than hiring a marketing consultant. Hiring a marketing apprentice or marketing assistant, if it works out, will give them an internal resource for the long-term. Hiring an agency will give them flexibility to scale up and down if they need to.

Some people really struggle with this because they're so convinced their business is the best choice for everyone. This isn't a bad thing — you're obviously very confident in your business! If this is you, just spend a bit of time on this and try to imagine yourself in the position of your ideal customer, who's never worked with you before, and has these choices laid out in front of them. The insights this exercise will give you are incredibly valuable. It's unlikely someone will end up as a happy customer if they come to you when there is actually a better alternative for them, and nothing builds trust like a business owner honestly acknowledging when they might not be the best choice for a potential customer.

A few years ago there was a TV advert for We Buy Any Car, showing a man playing football with his son. He's talking about how much he values his free time, which is why he likes We Buy Any Car. He says, "Sure, you might get a bit more money selling privately, but do you really need all that extra hassle? Wouldn't you rather get on with your day, like I'm doing?"

I love this advert because it calls out the biggest alternative and is honest about its advantages. We Buy Any Car knows exactly who their ideal customer is and why they want to use their service — people whose time is more valuable to them than the small amount of extra cash they could get selling privately. Anyone who's happy to do the legwork required to sell privately is welcome to go and do that. That's not the We Buy Any Car audience.

So think carefully about your ideal customer. What else might they consider doing to solve the problem they have?

This is often a great source of content. Write down both the advantages (to your customer) of choosing each alternative as well as the disadvantages and look for ideas for content you could create based on these themes.

A marketing consultant I know once wrote an article called, 'How much does a marketing consultant cost?' It was an honest, balanced article, explaining what you could expect from someone charging £300 a day, £600 a day and £1000 a day. She herself was charging at the upper end of that scale, so she wanted her prospects to know what to expect if they went to another consultant whose quote was much cheaper than hers. She didn't want people asking her for "£300-a-day" types of work, so it filtered out red-flag clients and prepared high-quality leads to expect the cost she was about to quote.

There might be good reasons why prospects would choose an alternative over your product or service, so be honest about it. Respect their choices, and you'll find yourself attracting much more loyal customers in the process.

YOUR PIXAR PITCH

If any of this section has been challenging for you, I encourage you to do this fun little exercise. It might seem silly, but it's surprisingly valuable and doesn't have to take long.

In Daniel Pink's book, *To Sell is Human*, he describes how Pixar always uses the same structure when pitching movie ideas. It goes like this:

- **Once upon a time ...**
- **Every day, ...**
- **One day, ...**
- **Because of that, ...**

- **Because of that, ...**
- **Until finally ...**

Pixar uses it to tell a compelling story in a short space of time, and I'll quote the example Pink uses here:

- **Once upon a time** there was a widowed fish named Marlin who was extremely protective of his only son, Nemo.
- **Every day,** Marlin warned Nemo of the ocean's dangers and implored him not to swim far away.
- **One day,** in an act of defiance, Nemo ignores his father's warnings and swims into the open water.
- **Because of that,** he is captured by a diver and ends up as a pet in the fish tank of a dentist in Sydney.
- **Because of that,** Marlin sets off on a journey to recover Nemo, enlisting the help of other sea creatures along the way.
- **Until finally** Marlin and Nemo find each other, reunite, and learn that love depends on trust.

Now it's your turn to create a Pixar Pitch for your ideal customer. Describe the story of your ideal customer and how they get value from your business. And you've already got all the basic elements:

- **Once upon a time** [Briefly describe your ideal customer]
- **Every day,** [Describe your "away from" and the challenges they're facing before they buy from you]
- **One day,** [What was the spark?]
- **Because of that,** [What action did they take as a result of the spark?]
- **Because of that,** [Describe the immediate benefits they saw]
- **Until finally** [Describe the "towards"and the ultimate benefits your customer has once they've got all the value you offer]

Have fun with it, and get creative.

To give you an example, here's one I wrote for a graphic design agency client:

- **Once upon a time** there was a marketing manager called Jane, whose job was to make her company's marketing happen.
- **Every day,** she wasted hours chasing up her design agency trying to get them to create the materials she needed.
- **One day,** the agency took so long and made so many mistakes that Jane missed her deadline and the whole campaign had to be scrapped.
- **Because of that,** Jane decided that there must be a better alternative and started looking into other graphic design agencies. She found one that worked efficiently and collaboratively with her to bring consistency to all her marketing collateral.
- **Because of that,** Jane had more time to be more creative with the execution of her marketing activities. She had more energy to develop effective campaigns and began to bring new, exciting marketing ideas to her company.
- **Until finally** her company saw how valuable her department's contribution was, so they increased her budget, responsibilities and salary. Without all the agency stress, Jane also began to enjoy her job again and rediscovered why she'd chosen that career in the first place.

And one that I wrote for my consultancy business with an engineering client in mind:

- **Once upon a time,** there was a managing director named Chris who ran a niche engineering consultancy.
- **Every day,** Chris and his team worked diligently on their complex services but struggled with marketing, because it just seemed to be "creative nonsense." Most customers came from word of mouth and exhibitions, but this wasn't enough to scale the business.
- **One day,** a business coach asked Chris, "How much have you spent on marketing, and how much are you getting back in sales?" Chris realised he had no control over his lead generation and no idea how his marketing spend would ever lead to sales.

- **Because of that,** Chris decided he needed a structured marketing strategy to deliver consistent leads and sales. He began working with The Marketing Machine Works, learning to target ideal customers, improve brand awareness, and effectively explain the company's niche services.
- **Because of that,** Chris and his team built solid marketing foundations and established a regular marketing rhythm that drove leads. With a measurable plan in place, Chris confidently hired a marketing manager to drive their marketing machine internally, supported by mentoring and training from The Marketing Machine Works.
- **Until finally,** Chris saw tangible results on his bottom line. The business grew, his employees thrived, and his marketing manager grew into a marketing superstar. Chris now had the headspace to drive the business forward, making strategic decisions with a clear path to scaling.

Have you got the idea? Now it's your turn.

Once you've written out your Pixar Pitch, go back through it and look for words and phrases that you'd like to use in your marketing. This is also a really good structure for a case study, although you may not want to start it with, "Once upon a time"!

DOES YOUR PROPOSITION MATCH YOUR IDEAL CUSTOMER?

Your customer persona and value proposition are like a roadmap and compass combined. They tell you exactly who you're speaking to, what they care about, and how you can help solve their problems or make their life easier.

As I said at the beginning of this chapter, your proposition and your ideal customer should be a perfect fit for each other. Look at them both side by side and assess whether they fit together. Does this person have these problems? Are these problems big enough that they're prepared to spend money fixing them? Is this person going to get the full benefit of all you have to offer?

If you know exactly who your audience is and that the value you offer is exactly what they need, then it will be natural for them to choose you over the alternatives.

It's difficult to answer the question of whether a proposition is "good enough". In truth, you can't answer that question without a big marketing research budget. But I always revert to my favourite mantra by Harry S. Truman: "Imperfect action is better than perfect inaction."

For most of the businesses I've worked with, the business owner knows the ideal customer pretty well, and they know enough about the real value they deliver to put together a decent proposition. Occasionally though, a business owner may feel unsure about their ideal customer and how that customer feels about the problem their business solves. They may not have worked with a particular audience for long and so may not know their audience's pain points very well. In these cases I usually recommend doing a little bit of market research, and you can find a whole lot more on this in Appendix 1 at the end of this book.

———

END OF CHAPTER CHECKLIST

I have:

☐ Identified my "Away from" pain points.

☐ Identified the Sparks that might trigger someone to start looking for what we offer.

☐ Identified my "Towards" messaging that describes the light at the end of the tunnel.

☐ Listed the alternatives someone might consider when purchasing from me, and the pros and cons of each option.

☐ Written my Pixar Pitch (optional, but recommended).

CHAPTER 5
MESSAGING THAT MOVES

As I said in the previous chapter, your value proposition isn't the same as a slogan or pithy soundbite for your website. But you do need to use your value proposition and ideal customer persona to create compelling messaging for your marketing.

So what do we do with all the work you've done so far? How and when do you use your "away from" and "towards" messaging? To answer this question, first you need to understand how our brains are wired.

HOW TO MAKE YOUR CUSTOMERS SIT UP AND TAKE NOTICE

In *The Chimp Paradox*, Prof. Steve Peters explains how we all have a primitive "chimp" brain as well as our rational "human" brain. These two brains have very different motivations and personalities. When we are relaxed, our human brain is in charge: it's the grown-up, rational, logical thinking part of our mind that makes decisions we are happy with. But when we are tired, stressed, angry or afraid, our Chimp brain wakes up and grabs the wheel.

The purpose of "The Chimp" is twofold: to keep us alive and to "ensure the next generation." It is responsible for our survival instincts: fight, flight, or freeze. When we're in one of these modes, our choices are often irrational. When our Chimp awakens to some perceived danger (which may not be real) and is trying to keep us alive, it can sometimes lead us to say or do things that aren't logical and may be out of character.

We want our customers to make logical choices they're happy with. I'm not in the business of creating marketing that sends people into a blind panic and leads to buyer's remorse. So everything I recommend in this book aims to keep your buyer's Chimp brain asleep so they can make a good, considered decision...

With one exception.

There's one moment in our buyer's journey when our Chimp brain can be useful. This is because the Chimp brain is quick to respond, and brilliant at getting us to take action. Its whole purpose is to alert us to danger and get us to move away to safety. Our Chimp brain responds quickly and instinctively, which is why it's important to speak to your customer's Chimp when you want them to sit up and take notice.

The first thing your audience sees — whether it's a headline, an ad, or a social media post — needs to be crafted to capture the attention of your customer's Chimp. That's why some of the most effective marketing headlines often focus on negative emotions or problems. These are the "away-from" messages: they speak to the fears, pain points, frustrations, and issues your customers want to avoid.

When a potential customer reads a headline that triggers a negative feeling or reminds them of a problem they have, their Chimp wakes up and says, "We need to fix this!" This is where your opportunity lies. The goal is to use this emotional trigger to make your message hit home.

For instance, if your business solves a particular problem your messaging should highlight that pain. For me, helping business owners manage marketing overwhelm, I might consider a headline like, 'Is Your Marketing Failing to Deliver Results?' or 'Three Costly Mistakes Every

Business Owner Makes with Their Marketing.' These speak directly to the Chimp. The negative emotion behind failing, making mistakes, or wasting time is a powerful motivator for action for the kinds of people I want to work with.

Once you've woken the Chimp, however, the last thing you want is for it to run wild looking for solutions elsewhere. This is where your "towards" messaging comes in — the reassuring, solution-focused part of your message. After highlighting the problem with your "away from" headline, immediately offer a solution and direct your customer to take the next step towards it. You're not just waking up the Chimp and leaving it in a panic; you're calming it straight away by presenting a clear path forward. In practical terms, this means that after an attention-grabbing headline, your subheading or the first sentence of your copy should immediately present the solution.

For example...

'Tired of managing endless paperwork?'
Streamline your process with our easy-to-use automation tools.

'Struggling to find the right talent for your team?'
Connect with top candidates faster using our advanced recruitment platform.

'Struggling with slow software performance?'
Optimise your systems with our performance-boosting tools.

'Is your home office killing your productivity?'
Transform your workspace with our free design checklist.

'Losing track of project progress and deadlines?'
Keep your projects on track with our real-time monitoring and collaboration platform.

Testimonials that speak to the emotional benefits of your solution also work really well in this "towards" space. For example, I have a client testimonial that says, "It's taken away a stress and a doubt" that I often use underneath an "away from" headline. The testimonial resonates deeply with others feeling the same stress and doubt, and it reassures the buyer's Chimp that they are in the right place, looking at the solution they need.

By addressing both the problem (the away-from message) and the solution (the towards message) in quick succession, you give your audience's Chimp a problem to solve and an immediate sense of relief. This is crucial because once the Chimp feels reassured, the rational part of the brain can take over and process the value of your offer, allowing the buyer to make a considered decision.

BUILDING YOUR MESSAGING TOOLBOX WITH... CLICKBAIT!

I love clickbait. I know I may be the only person in the world to say this, but it's true. If you're stuck on how to craft a great headline, one of the best places to look for inspiration is clickbait.

If you've never heard the term, clickbait is the name for a headline so compelling you just have to click on it... which then takes you to an underwhelming article full of advertising that is purely designed to generate revenue for the website.

The reason clickbait works is because it's brilliant at waking up the Chimp. It's very cleverly designed to provoke an emotional reaction — whether it's curiosity, fear, or excitement — that makes us click.

Take a look at clickbait headlines like, 'The One Mistake That's Ruining Your Finances,' or 'You Won't Believe What Happened When She Tried This Diet.' These types of headlines are carefully structured to grab attention quickly and make people feel like they *have* to click to find out more. It's that emotional pull, that spark of curiosity or fear, that makes the Chimp react.

Of course, I'm not suggesting you create headlines baiting your customers towards low-quality content — quite the opposite! But you can use a similar structure in your headlines to prompt your customers to notice what you're offering them. For example, using the above headlines as inspiration, I could write an article called, 'The One Mistake That's Killing Your Marketing Results', or 'You Won't Believe What Happened When She Tried This Marketing Trick.'

OK, that second one really doesn't suit me, and I probably wouldn't use it unless it was a tongue-in-cheek post for social media, but you can see the point I'm making here.

When you create headlines that follow these patterns, you're not tricking people — you're speaking directly to the part of their brain that *needs* to know more. Whether it's a blog post, a sales page, or an email subject line, using these headline structures can drive more engagement and action from your audience. Just make sure your content delivers on the promise. You can find a list of clickbait headline structures on the resources page for this book.[1]

As you develop your messaging, it's a good idea to start building a 'bank' of headlines and phrases that you can use across your marketing efforts. Begin by brainstorming headlines that provoke the Chimp, and think about how they could be adapted for different platforms and media — your website, blogs, social media, videos, email campaigns, or advertising.

Once you've got your bank of away-from and towards messages, you'll be prepared to capture attention and guide your customers toward action.

MARKET RESEARCH

As I mentioned at the end of the last chapter, if you're not completely sure about your audience yet, a little market research can save you a lot of time and money.

Market research is all about gathering and analysing information to better understand your audience. It doesn't need to be complicated, just

---

1. https://rosconkie.com/TheMarketingMachineResources

enough to understand what's going on in your customers' minds — especially if you need some help figuring out what wakes up their Chimp.

Market research is most commonly used when businesses are stepping into unfamiliar territory, like exploring a new market or targeting a different audience. However, it's also especially useful if you're feeling unsure about your customers' pain points or if your current assumptions need a reality check. If articulating your ideal customer persona feels like a struggle or you're unclear about what makes your offering stand out, investing time in a little bit of research can provide the clarity you need. Ultimately, understanding your audience not only helps tailor your marketing strategies but also boosts your chances of building lasting customer relationships.

If this is something you need to do, I've put a detailed description of how to undertake a simple market research project in Appendix 1.

———

END OF CHAPTER CHECKLIST

I have:

☐ Identified the triggers that wake up my ideal customer's Chimp brain.

☐ Built my messaging toolbox with attention-grabbing headline ideas and Chimp-pacifying subheading ideas.

☐ Decided whether market research is needed.

CHAPTER 6

MAPPING YOUR BUYER JOURNEY

Continuing with our design process, you now know what raw materials are going into your marketing machine (your ideal customer), and what the engine of the machine will be (the value proposition that drives the customer to buy). Now we need to design how those elements will combine to be transformed into your output: a long-term, profitable customer.

How does an ideal customer who's never heard of you before become a happy, loyal customer who gets loads of value and tells all their friends about you?

This is what I call the "buyer journey".

The aim of marketing and sales is to take people on a journey from knowing nothing about you to being a "raving fan" who buys loyally and tells all their friends. Some people call this a funnel or a pipeline, but there's a good reason I don't use these words. The words "funnel" and "pipeline" are only useful to describe the process if we look at it from *your* perspective. I very much doubt any customer would like to feel they're in a funnel or a pipeline. This should not describe your customer's experience of the process. It may seem pedantic, but if we use these words then it subtly tells our brain to bring our focus back to our own perspective. If you want to keep yourself focused on your customers — to ensure they can buy from you easily and comfortably — then I strongly recommend you use words that facilitate this.

To make it really easy for people to buy, you need to understand how your customers make the journey from being completely unaware of you to being a loyal customer and, if possible, referring you to other people. The journey will be different depending on your ideal customer and your proposition.

But before we start designing your buyer journey, we need to understand how long your customer's journey is. This is dependent on your buyer's perceived risk.

WHAT IS THE RISK OF BUYING?

We're all able to live with a degree of risk in our lives, but how much will vary from person to person. Some people are risk-takers and are willing to live with a higher degree of risk. These people are often happy making high-risk, high-reward investments. Other people are more risk-averse and will tend to choose options that are a safe bet.

If your product or service looks like a high-risk purchase, then you'll never sell to someone who's risk-averse. You might still sell to the risk-takers because they'll see the value of what you're offering and will feel like the risk is worth it, but risk-averse people will struggle to buy in.

Marketing is all about reducing the perceived risk of buying and to build trust so that it's easy for everyone to buy, whatever their risk tolerance.

It's important to note here that the word "perceived" is important. This is not about actual risk — it's only about the customer's perception of risk. You might have a guarantee in place that means the actual risk of the purchase is zero, but the customer doesn't know whether you'd honour it. They don't know if there's a hidden clause in the T&Cs that you'd quibble over, or if you're a scammer who's planning to take their money and disappear.

So, looking at your business from your customer's perspective, what's the risk of buying from you? Maybe they look at what you sell and think, "If I make the wrong choice it doesn't matter too much. It's not a lot of money so the worst case is I'll be a little out of pocket. No big deal."

Or maybe they look at your products and services and think, "I need to take my time making this decision because if I make the wrong choice, then I'll lose a lot of money and waste a lot of time."

It may feel discouraging to focus on risk at this point, but that feeling of risk is what stops people from throwing their credit card at you when you tell them what you do. If you've ever wondered why sales are slow, or why people seem reluctant to buy from you when you know that they'd get so much value from your offering, the answer is likely around perceived risk.

For example, if a business manager chooses a bad IT software system for their company then all their colleagues will blame them for making their lives harder. Worse, that decision will also annoy their boss, which could risk their promotion and possibly even their career. That's a high-risk purchase!

The great news is that if you really, deeply understand your customer's perceived risk then you can put marketing assets in place to build trust and reduce that perceived risk. We'll get on to exactly how to do this later on, but for now, put yourself back in your customer's mind, and start thinking about how much risk your customer might perceive there to be in the decision to buy from you.

As I said before, if your product or service looks risky from your customer's perspective, then you're limiting your sales potential. You'll still probably make some sales because some people are risk-takers, but you'll have a hard time selling to more risk-averse buyers.

If you're not sure what this difference feels like to a customer, head over to eBay. Find a product listing with one grainy photo, no seller rating and almost no information about the product. How do you feel when you consider buying it? A bit uncomfortable? Maybe there's something in your gut telling you to walk away? What if you spend that money and then discover the item is damaged when it arrives? What if it doesn't arrive at all and you have to waste ages trying to get a refund?

To contrast this, look for a listing with lots of photos of the product, a detailed description and a large number of five-star reviews for the seller. Doesn't this give you more confidence? It could be the same product at the same price, but the listing which reduces the perceived risk will sell a lot more because it feels less risky.

If your marketing is going to make it really easy for customers to buy from you, then you need to reduce the perceived risk of buying.

The level of perceived risk will affect how long your customer's buyer journey is and how much support they'll need on that journey. If the perceived risk is quite low then you may have a relatively short buyer journey. If the perceived risk is higher, you'll have a longer buyer journey.

So how risky is it to buy from you? The best way to think about this is to consider the impact to your buyer if they make a bad buying decision.

Remember, they've never bought from you before. They don't know that you're actually brilliant. They can only see your business from the outside, and we all have a healthy level of scepticism. Put yourself back in your customer's mind again and imagine you know nothing about your business. What is the impact of making a bad buying decision?

There are a few things to consider here.

Money

How significant is the cost to your buyer? Cost is relative of course — for some people £100 is a fortune and for other people it's pocket change. People's attitudes to investment are also greatly affected by whose money they are spending and where it came from. Consider whether the money is their own hard-earned cash or whether it's part of a large budget allocated to them by the company they work for.

Think about your audience and their budget. The risk here is that the person buying will lose their money. How would they perceive losing the cost of your product or service?

Time

How much time will your customer need to invest before they will get value from what you offer?

For example, a new IT system may take a lot of time to set up before the customer will get value from it. What if things go wrong? How much time will it take them to put things right again? What if the IT system turns out to be terrible and they have to spend ages undoing all that work?

The risk here is that the person will waste their time. How much time could be lost and how valuable is your customer's time to them? If they live a relatively busy life, have a high-powered career, or have other significant time constraints in their life, then wasting time will increase the perceived risk of buying from you. On the other hand, if your ideal customer is retired and has more leisure time then they may not be so concerned about wasting time.

Impact on relationships

Let's stay with the example of the IT system. Once implemented, it would likely affect the customer's whole company and everyone in it. If the business manager makes a bad buying decision it could make them very unpopular. Perhaps their boss might start to doubt their ability to make good decisions, so they may not be trusted with other important decisions any more. A bad buying decision could damage their reputation and even their career prospects.

If the decision could impact many people then that increases the perceived risk of buying. Equally, if the decision could impact people who are especially important to the customer, then that also gives us pause for thought. For example, if I buy a special gift for my spouse and they hate it, I'll feel awful. If I buy a toy for my child and it turns out to be poor quality and puts their health or safety at risk, I'll be devastated.

Again, put yourself in your customer's shoes. What relationships could be impacted by a bad buying decision when it comes to your product or service?

Complexity

Some buying decisions are simple. I know what kind of milk I like, so I just buy it. I need one specific type of lightbulb, so I buy that one. There's very little to think about.

For other decisions there's a lot to think about — things like house purchases and company acquisitions. When buying a house there are so many things to think about, and we may also need to educate ourselves about the decision if we've not bought something like this before. Asking price, size, style, location, garden (or lack of one), garage (or lack of one), number of rooms, condition of the building, scale of any renovations, proximity to schools and work, and many more. In most situations, people will naturally take their time with this decision. Choosing the wrong house — or paying too much for the right one — is a huge risk.

When a buying process involves a lot of people, as you might see in purchases between companies, this also adds complexity. When the purchase has to be signed off by multiple people, not only is the perceived risk impacted by the relationships between the people, as I mentioned above, but each of those people will have their own concerns and agendas that all need to be resolved and aligned.

The combination of risks

In the previous chapter I described my husband and I choosing a home security system. It was a meaningful amount of money, but we considered it worthwhile given the stress of dealing with the burglary. My husband planned to install the system himself, so we considered how much time it would take him before we'd be able to use it. This decision would impact both of us, as well as our children (i.e. multiple important relationships). The decision felt very complex because there were so many different technologies and options for us to consider.

With all these things in mind, go back to your customer's point of view and think about how much of a risk it is to buy from you.

HOW LONG IS YOUR CUSTOMER'S BUYER JOURNEY?

In general, the lower the perceived risk of buying, the shorter the buyer journey. The higher the risk, the longer (and slower) the buyer journey.

At the low-risk end of the scale, we have "impulse buys". Imagine there's a new drink on the market (I'll leave you to decide what kind of drink!). First you'd have been unaware of the product. Then perhaps you saw an advert and became interested in trying it. Then you saw it in a shop or restaurant or bar, and decided to try it. If you loved it, you might start buying it regularly.

In that instance there were four recognisable stages:

1. Unaware
2. Interested
3. Test purchase
4. Loyal customer

At the high-risk end of the scale, there may be more stages for the customer to go through. With some of my clients we can identify eight or nine stages. For example, when people hear about my consulting and training business for the first time, they may not immediately see the value of getting external marketing support. And if they do, they often take a bit of time to think about it. From talking to customers, I've realised they often think to themselves, "Yes, we do need to sort out our marketing at some point. But I have too much going on right now — I need to finish this project/busy season/HR challenge first before I can think about it." They mentally file us away as something that may be useful to them in the future, but not right now.

At some point, something happens (one of the "sparks" we looked at earlier) and they realise that marketing is now a priority for them and they are interested to find out more. They might read some of my content and watch some of my videos, alongside investigating other alternatives. When they've decided that this is definitely a priority and it's the right time, they'll narrow down their options and book a call with me.

On our call we'll talk about what they need and how I might be able to help them. I'll usually offer a small initial piece of work that will give them plenty of value and will give us both the opportunity to check we're a good fit to work together. When they're happy with what they've got from that test purchase, I'll offer something else and, assuming they're happy to continue, we'll keep working together. After a while they'll feel so happy with the work we're doing that they wouldn't want to go anywhere else. Eventually, they may write a testimonial or recommend us to someone they know.

I can map all this behaviour into these recognisable stages:

1. Unaware
2. Aware
3. Filed for later
4. Interested in finding out more
5. Seriously considering/narrowing down options
6. Test purchase
7. Bought in
8. Loyal
9. Referring

Every business and every ideal customer persona will have a slightly different buyer journey. This is why copying other people's marketing activities doesn't work. If you've ever looked at someone else's marketing and wondered why it works so well in their business but not in yours, this is why.

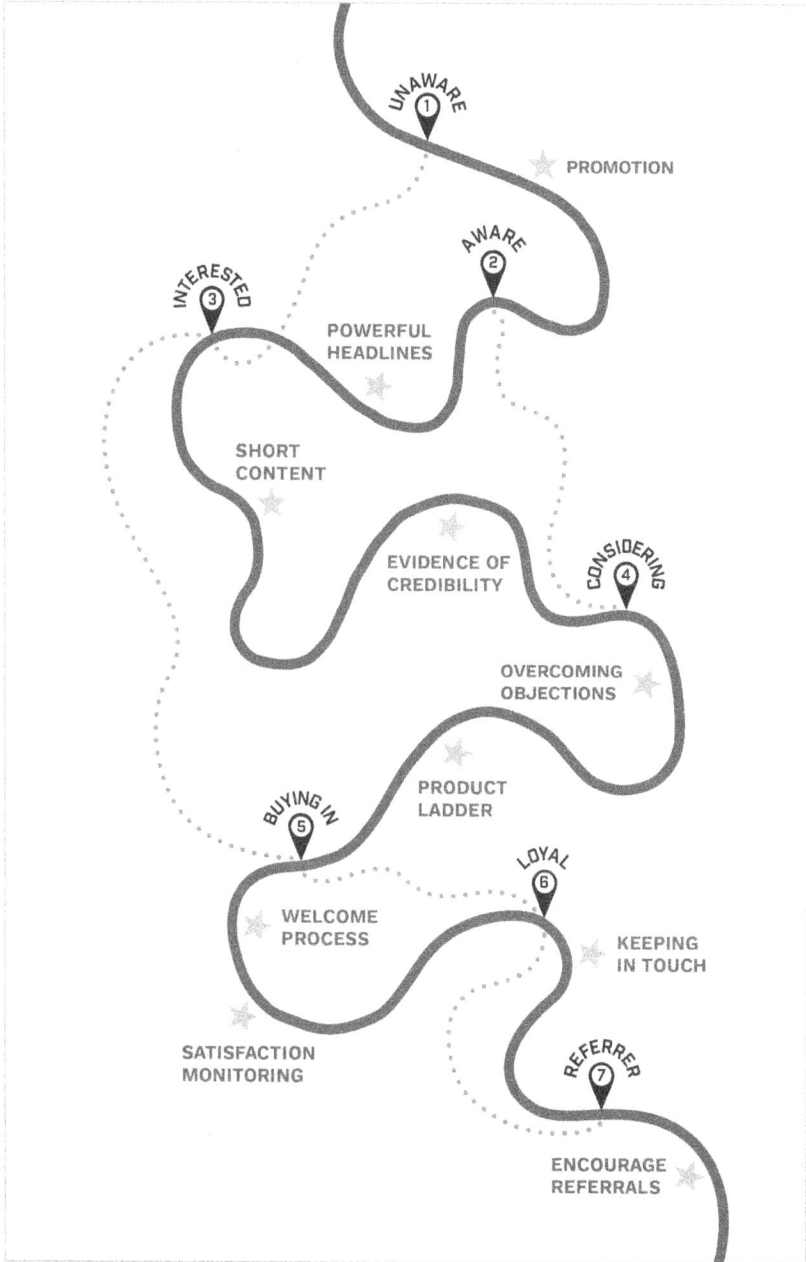

A long buyer journey: from Unaware to Referrer and beyond

Your marketing machine should move your customers from the "unaware" stage to the "loyal" stage (where they're most profitable), and preferably to "referrer", where they start generating business for you. To do that, you'll need to support your buyers at every stage of their buying process and encourage them on to the next stage.

But how do you do that in practice? The first step is to map out your own buyer journey.

HOW TO MAP OUT YOUR CURRENT BUYER JOURNEY

Since every business has a different ideal customer and therefore a different buyer journey, you need to map yours. I want you to map out your buyer journey as it is right now, and we will then use it to identify ways you can better support your customers. You may already have a mental list of things you want to add, and you may find that this process quickly gives you some ideas for improvement as well. If that happens, put those ideas in a separate place for now and we'll add them to your buyer journey later.

How long is your buyer journey? Is it quite short or is it long? It could be similar to one of the two I've mapped out above, it could be in between... or possibly even longer than mine!

What stages can you recognise in that decision-making process? You may like to name the stages similarly to mine or you may prefer to tailor the words to better fit your journey. You may want to substitute "test purchase" for "receive a quote", or it may make more sense in your business to substitute "seriously considering" for "contact service provider". You may not have a "filed for later" stage at all and other stages may be merged or moved around. This journey has to fit your business.

As I've said, it's essential to keep your ideal customer in mind while you do this. If you're not sure, it can be useful to watch your customers' behaviour for a while and possibly ask them as well.

When you're doing this, you may find yourself thinking about the outliers who bought from you very quickly or those who bought particularly slowly. In every business there'll be some customers who skip through their buying decision very quickly — maybe they're quite risk-taking personalities, maybe the risks aren't so great for them, or maybe it's an emergency purchase. It doesn't matter if people choose to take short-cuts. The objective of your marketing is to make it as easy as possible for as many people as possible to buy from you, and that includes the risk-averse customers. For this exercise, think about the customers who take a bit more time than average: not the quickest or the very slowest, but those who were just a bit on the slower side of normal.

If you're in doubt about whether to include a particular stage, err on the side of caution and include it. If you lay down more steps for your customer than they need, they'll just skip over them. But if you don't have enough steps laid out for your risk-averse customers, they'll choose not to buy and you won't get as many sales as you could.

If you're completely at a loss of how many stages you might have, start with the stages I used above for the long buyer journey and, as you get into the process of mapping, take out stages if they seem irrelevant.

What you're aiming to achieve is a kind of diagram showing all the ways people might interact with and be supported by your business through each of the stages of their decision-making process. There's an example of a completed buyer journey on the next page.

When you create yours, don't worry if it looks a bit sparse at this stage. We'll go through all the ways you can improve your buyer journey later in this book.

Let's get started!

For this exercise, I've created a Google Slides template for you to use which you can download from rosconkie.com/TheMarketingMachine Resources. I suggest reading through this process before you start actually working through it — it's quite detailed and it will be easier to execute if you've seen the whole process before you get started.

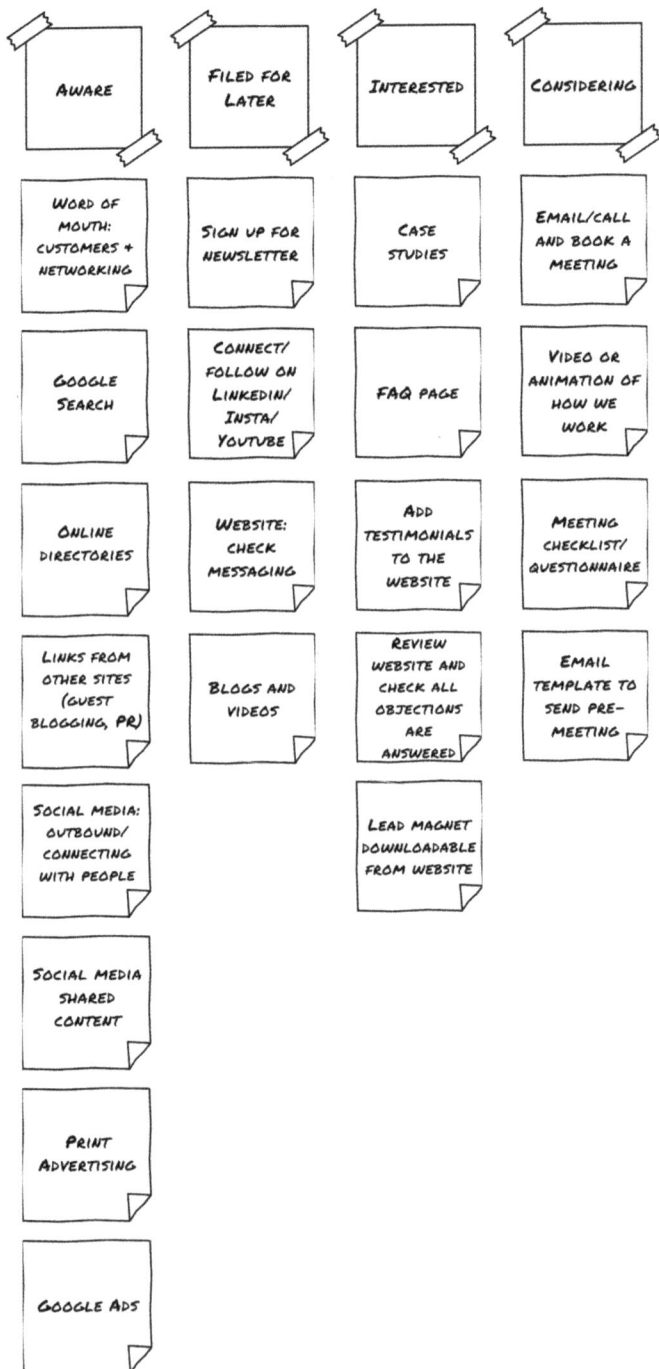

AWARE	FILED FOR LATER	INTERESTED	CONSIDERING
WORD OF MOUTH: CUSTOMERS + NETWORKING	SIGN UP FOR NEWSLETTER	CASE STUDIES	EMAIL/CALL AND BOOK A MEETING
GOOGLE SEARCH	CONNECT/ FOLLOW ON LINKEDIN/ INSTA/ YOUTUBE	FAQ PAGE	VIDEO OR ANIMATION OF HOW WE WORK
ONLINE DIRECTORIES	WEBSITE: CHECK MESSAGING	ADD TESTIMONIALS TO THE WEBSITE	MEETING CHECKLIST/ QUESTIONNAIRE
LINKS FROM OTHER SITES (GUEST BLOGGING, PR)	BLOGS AND VIDEOS	REVIEW WEBSITE AND CHECK ALL OBJECTIONS ARE ANSWERED	EMAIL TEMPLATE TO SEND PRE-MEETING
SOCIAL MEDIA: OUTBOUND/ CONNECTING WITH PEOPLE		LEAD MAGNET DOWNLOADABLE FROM WEBSITE	
SOCIAL MEDIA SHARED CONTENT			
PRINT ADVERTISING			
GOOGLE ADS			

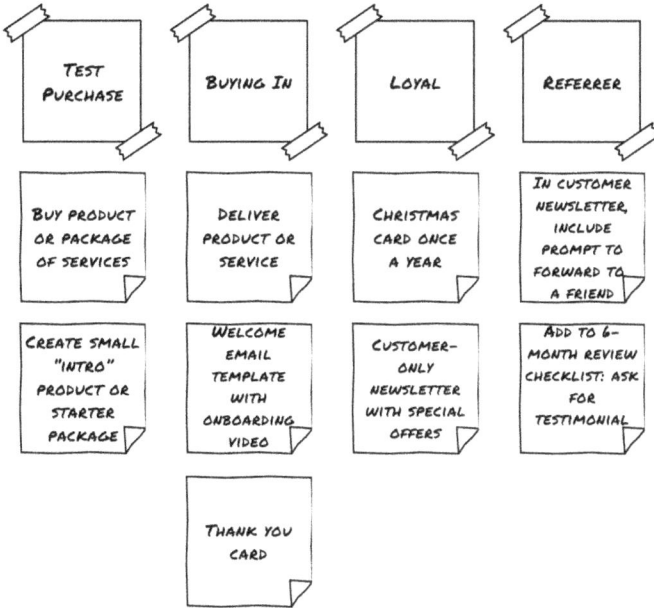

If you're a "pen and paper" person, you're welcome to use a big piece of paper with post-its, or a whiteboard. And if you're Google-averse, Miro and Canva also work well.

On my Google Slides template, you'll see a worked example of a buyer journey, and an empty template for you to create your own, using colour-coded digital post-its that you can move around.

Start by writing out the stages of your buyer journey in order along the top of your slide, leaving space underneath to put the activities you have in place at each stage.

Most businesses start at "Aware" and finish at "Referrer". As I said, if you're in doubt, start with the following (long) journey. As you go through the process of mapping your journey out, if you decide that one of the stages isn't relevant to your buyer then just take it out.

The 'long' buyer journey I usually start with is:

- Aware
- Filed for later
- Interested
- Considering
- Test purchase
- Buying in
- Loyal
- Referrer

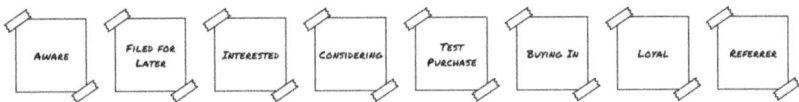

We're going to map out your *existing* buyer journey first, leaving any ideas you have for the future to one side for now. We're going to mark out the activities, processes and content that support your customers at each stage of the journey as it currently works.

Start at the beginning of your journey. Write down on separate post-its all the ways your customers could hear about you for the very first time (the green ones, if you're using the template). Put one idea on each post-it and arrange them in a column below your "Aware" stage label.

Bear in mind that your website will almost never be a first point of contact. The rare exception is if it's such an obvious URL that someone might conceivably type it in before they've heard of you (e.g. hotels.-com). In all likelihood, they'll come via search first, or a referral from another website, or some other mechanism. Ask yourself: how do they hear about your business?

Most businesses will have a number of different ways customers will hear about them for the first time.

You might have things like referrals from customers, search engines, meeting at networking events, print advertising, Google Ads, PR, events, hashtags on Instagram, searches on LinkedIn, Facebook adverts... etc. There are a lot of ways people can hear about you.

It's important to be specific here. "Social media" is too vague. For a start, which platform(s) will they find you on? How do they find you? Remember that people will probably only see your posts if they're following you, so that won't be how they *first* hear about you. Unaware people might see a post that their friend has shared or liked — does that drive traffic to your business? If you use hashtags or paid advertising, that will get in front of unaware people too. On LinkedIn, for example, people might hear about you because you searched and found them and connected with them. Or did you find them and comment on their post? Whatever the mechanisms are for your business, be specific.

Then ask yourself: what will they do next? Do they go to your website next? Maybe they go to your LinkedIn profile or your Facebook page? Do they read about you on your website? What are they looking for?

When and how do they first make contact with you? How do they flag up to you that they exist and may be interested in what you have to offer? Do they phone or email you? Do they fill in a form or download a piece of content? Do they come and visit your showroom or shop? In my experience, people make contact with businesses much later now than we used to because we're hesitant about being hounded by over-zealous email automations. So at what point do your customers first make contact?

And then what happens?

Do they have a meeting with you? Do you send them a quote or a proposal?

At some point they'll buy from you, so what marketing and customer service do you do at that point?

And then what do you do afterwards?

Keep going until you have mapped out all the activities, resources and processes you currently have in place.

Here's a full breakdown of everything I have listed in my example buyer journey:

- Aware:
  - Word of mouth
  - Google search
  - Online directories and review websites
  - Links from other sites
  - Social media outbound (making connections)
  - Social media shared content
- Filed for later:
  - Sign up for our newsletter
  - Connect/follow on LinkedIn, Instagram and YouTube
- Interested:
  - Case studies
  - FAQ page
- Considering:
  - A call to action on the website saying, "Email or call us and book a meeting."
- Test purchase:
  - The option to buy a product or package of services.

- Buying in:
  - At this stage we just deliver our product or service — we don't have anything else to support our customers here.
- Loyal:
  - We send a Christmas card once a year.
- Referrer
  - No support here yet.

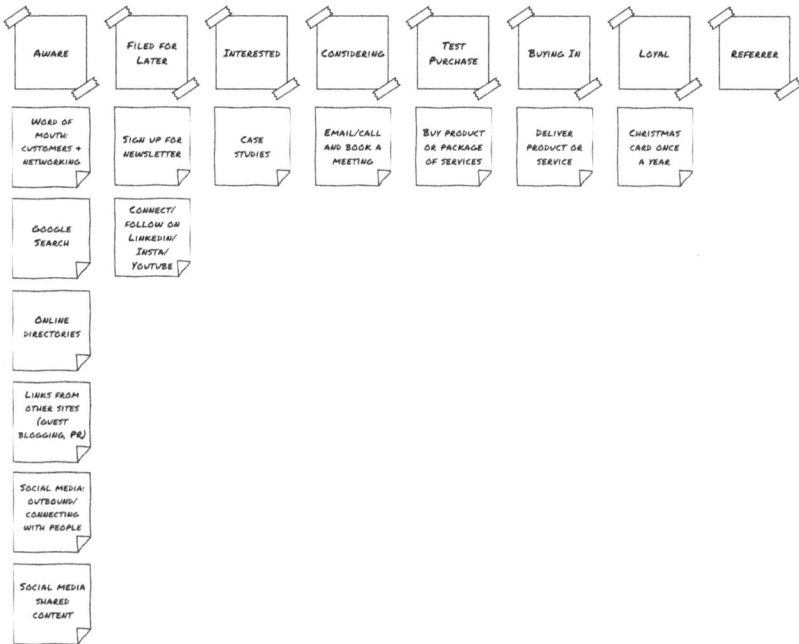

If you already have marketing activities in mind that you haven't yet implemented, write those on red post-its and copy them to an empty slide for now.

We'll add these red post-its back in later, when we look at all the ways you can improve your buyer journey and, at that point, we'll prioritise them alongside your new ideas. At the moment, we don't know how high a priority they are, and it's easy to get distracted by marketing ideas that turn out to be low priorities.

If you have any marketing activities that are in progress but not yet complete, add them onto your buyer journey on orange post-its.

Now you've mapped out your buyer journey, take a step back and look at it. Don't worry if you have stages with no marketing currently happening to support customers there. That's normal — and it's actually good news! Every gap in your marketing machine is an opportunity to increase your sales. In the chapter called 'Optimising Your Buyer Journey', I'll explain lots of different ways you can support people better at every stage of their buying decision. In 'Prioritise, Plan, Propel', we'll cover how to work out which task to start with and in what order to implement your marketing ideas.

By the end of this book you'll know exactly what you need to do to plug all those gaps. And once you've plugged them, your customers will find it much easier to buy from you, which will naturally lead to more sales.

———

END OF CHAPTER CHECKLIST

I have:

☐ Identified the risks my buyer might perceive in their decision.

☐ Identified the stages of my buyer journey.

☐ Mapped out my current buyer journey.

CHAPTER 7
MEASURE AND TEST

Have you ever felt that small but persistent doubt that the time and money you've spent on marketing might not have been worth it? If you want to be completely confident in your marketing, then measuring it is absolutely essential.

Measurement is one of the most important but overlooked aspects of any successful marketing strategy. This is for a number of reasons:

1. It's difficult to know where to start with measurement, so lots of people just don't start at all.
2. People try to measure everything at once, get overwhelmed, lose momentum and stop.
3. Some metrics are extremely useful, and others are really not useful at all. You need to understand the difference in order to make decisions about what can be improved or what to change going forwards.
4. Many people believe it's impossible to effectively measure your marketing. John Wanamaker, a nineteenth-century marketing pioneer, said, "Half the money I spend on advertising is wasted; the trouble is, I don't know which half." In the

twenty-first century people still assume this applies to their own marketing.

I believe these reasons are why marketing often gets a bad reputation: marketers fail to effectively measure their activities and demonstrate the results.

I'll hold my hands up right now and say that I made this mistake more times than I'd like to admit in the past, because I didn't have the structure and process for measurement that I have now. When you're not measuring effectively, you're essentially turning your marketing investment into a game of luck.

So, how can you turn your marketing from a gamble into a predictable, replicable system? How often should you be measuring to get useful results that'll inform your marketing strategy moving forward? And how can you know that you're getting a return on your marketing investment? Let's dive into how you can measure your marketing effectively, while keeping it realistic and manageable for a small business.

THE BIGGEST MEASUREMENT MISTAKE

The biggest mistake business owners make in marketing is thinking of their marketing as one big thing that's either working or not working.

Imagine you need a car. You spend months designing and building it. You finally put the key in the ignition to go for a drive and... nothing happens.

Do you...

A. Scrap the car and design a new one?
B. Look at each of the individual components in the car, testing and measuring each one, to try and work out which part is broken?

I hope the answer's pretty obvious!

It doesn't take a mechanic to see that there could be a hundred reasons why the car isn't working.

Maybe the starter motor isn't connected. Maybe it's got no fuel. Maybe you've got the wrong key! There could be literally hundreds of reasons that it's not working.

But when people try marketing activities, they often see them all as being one thing that's either working or not working. In reality, your marketing is made up of many components which each need to be tested and measured in order to make the whole machine run as efficiently as possible.

Look back at your buyer journey, and remember that the purpose of marketing is to help people move from one end to the other. Each individual component of your marketing machine is there to move someone from one stage of the journey to the next. So our goal with measurement is to check that each component is doing this effectively.

Measuring the components is not about 'reach' or clicks or followers or page-views. It's about measuring how effectively your marketing is converting people from one stage in the journey to the next.

People say things like...

"I tried Instagram, but it didn't work."

"I tried Google Ads, but I didn't get any sales from it."

"I tried exhibitions, but they were a waste of money."

Then they ask me what they're doing wrong in their marketing, as if their whole marketing machine is broken. Invariably, the machine itself isn't a complete write-off. Instead, there will be loads of things that can be improved. The challenge is identifying which cog needs some grease, which one's a bit wonky, and which ones are missing altogether.

At this stage, you know who you're trying to attract to your business. You know why they'd buy from you, and how they're going to become a customer. That means that you can test and measure each component of your marketing machine to check that it's working efficiently to achieve the results you want.

IS MARKETING JUST A NUMBERS GAME?

The short answer is yes, but not in the way most people think.

When people say that marketing is a numbers game, what they usually mean is that they need to generate as many leads as possible so they can sell as much as they can. Quite often, business owners make the mistake of believing that this means they need to get more followers, or send out more emails, or spend more on advertising.

While lead generation is obviously an important part of marketing, it's not actually the most important number to be concerned about. If you're not looking at other metrics, like your conversion rates, then you can waste a lot of time and money.

Anyone with a little marketing experience can spend lots of your money generating more leads. But if you're not looking at the other, more important numbers in your business, then you'll never be as profitable as you can be.

I should probably give a slight health-warning at this point because, although I work with a lot of engineers and spreadsheet-minded people, I've had many maths-phobic clients too. I promise I'll keep this as simple as possible but, inevitably, there's a bit of maths involved. If, when reading this chapter, you reach your limit for maths tolerance, hand this chapter to a trusted advisor, CFO, fractional financial director or a good accountant and work through it with their help. If you're struggling to visualise this, I have a video tutorial on my website that explains this process.[1]

So, is your marketing as profitable as it could be? Effective measurement will tell you the answer.

---

1. https://rosconkie.com/TheMarketingMachineResources

WHAT SHOULD I BE MEASURING?

The wonderful thing about marketing now (compared to when I started working in the industry 20 years ago) is that we have so much data at our fingertips. The downside is also that we have *so* much data at our fingertips.

Marketing data is a deep and twisty rabbit hole that's extremely easy to fall into. I've worked with many customers who've tried to mine their data for useful insights, only to fall into the hole, drag themselves out, and run away screaming. I myself have fallen into the hole many times!

The difficulty is keeping your measurements as simple as possible while also getting enough data to provide valuable insights. Fortunately, it's possible to get incredibly valuable insights from small amounts of data — you just need the *right* data.

WHAT'S THE RIGHT DATA? AND WHAT'S THE WRONG DATA?

The most important metrics you can measure are your conversion rates. Conversion rates tell you where your marketing is working and where there are opportunities to improve.

You may already be familiar with using the phrase "conversion rate" to describe how many leads turn into sales. This is a good place to start, but if this is the only conversion rate you're measuring then it doesn't help you improve your marketing. When you start measuring your conversion rates along your entire buyer journey, that's when you discover which elements of your marketing machine are working well and which components need improving.

A conversion rate is the percentage of customers who successfully move from one step in your buyer journey to the next. For example, to see how successful a landing page on your website is, you'd look at the percentage of visitors to the page who click on your 'call to action' button. If 10 out of every 100 visitors to your page click on the button, your conversion rate is 10%.

Luckily, you've already mapped out your buyer journey, and we'll come back to this soon to look at all the possible conversion points a customer will go through.

Let's say your business currently gets 20 enquiries per month and those enquiries turn into five new customers. If you want to double your business, you have two options:

1. Generate 40 enquiries per month.
2. Convert twice as many enquiries into customers.

Most of the work that increases conversion rates involves things like improving processes and creating evergreen content that makes it easier for people to buy from you. These things only need to be done once and then all prospective customers will benefit. In short, Option 2 will involve a one-off investment to increase your conversion rate, but after that you would expect to see an increase in sales revenue for the same monthly spend.

Option 1, on the other hand, means you will have to spend a lot more on marketing every single month forever.

So do you want to spend twice as much on marketing every month, or do you want to invest in your marketing once, then spend the same amount and get twice the return?

The other problem with only increasing lead generation without watching the conversion rates is that a lot of marketing is not actually as scalable as it looks. Doubling your Google Ads spend, for example, doesn't always get twice as many potential customers to your website. Sometimes it does, but it's not guaranteed.

SO, HOW DO I MEASURE MY CONVERSION RATES?

Most of my customers measure a number of different conversion rates:

- How many people who see your Google Ad click on the link?

- How many website visitors book a call?
- How many calls with new prospects result in a proposal or quote being sent out?
- How many proposals result in sales?

Tracking numbers like these will tell you where your marketing investment is making an impact and where you're losing customers along the journey.

Go back to your buyer journey now and look at how you might measure someone at each stage of your buyer journey. You'll probably find that some stages are easier than others: if that's the case, just focus on measuring the ones you can easily measure and, for now, don't worry about the tricky ones.

Here's an example of a buyer journey where four stages can easily be measured. In this example, the buyer journey starts with a LinkedIn connection, but your buyer journey might start with a Google search, or a digital advert or a referral or any other marketing activity. The process is the same regardless.

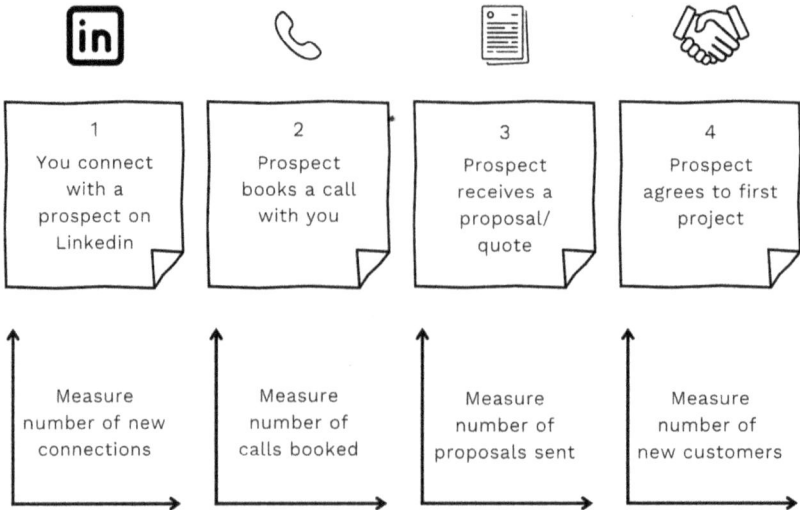

1	2	3	4
You connect with a prospect on Linkedin	Prospect books a call with you	Prospect receives a proposal/ quote	Prospect agrees to first project

| Measure number of new connections | Measure number of calls booked | Measure number of proposals sent | Measure number of new customers |

Now you've chosen your metrics, you can start measuring how many people you have at each stage. Depending on your business, you might choose to measure on a weekly, monthly or quarterly basis.

Let's imagine in this example you're measuring monthly, so each month you'll tally up the number of new connections you made on LinkedIn this month, the number of calls you had with new prospects, the number of proposals you sent out and the number of new customers you had this month.

Let's imagine these are your metrics for this month. You can use these measurements to work out your conversion rates from each stage to the next one:

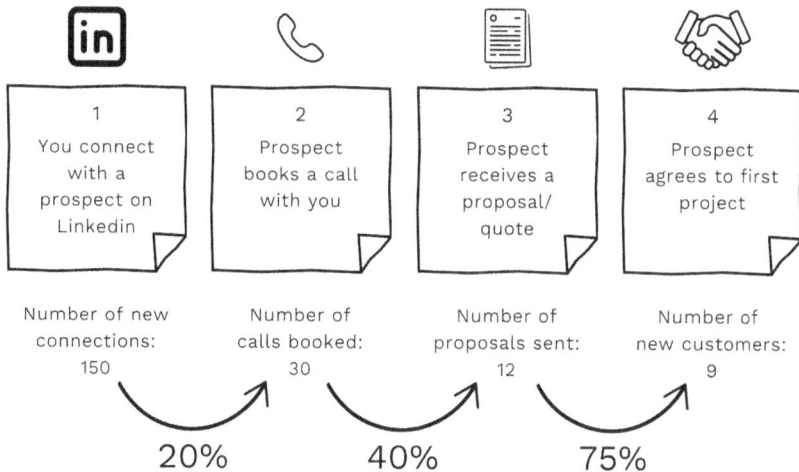

1	2	3	4
You connect with a prospect on Linkedin	Prospect books a call with you	Prospect receives a proposal/quote	Prospect agrees to first project
Number of new connections: 150	Number of calls booked: 30	Number of proposals sent: 12	Number of new customers: 9

20%   40%   75%

This month you connected with 150 people on LinkedIn. 30 people booked a call with you, so your conversion rate from connection to call is 20%. 12 people asked for a proposal so your conversion rate from call to proposal is 40%. And finally, nine people became new customers by agreeing to a first project, so your conversion rate from proposal to customer is 75%.

If you've never measured any of your marketing activities before, I recommend you start exactly like this example above. Pick three or four points on your buyer journey where you can easily measure people on the buyer journey. Start measuring and, once you have some data, work out your conversion rates.

As you get used to this process of measuring, you'll want to measure more stages of your buyer journey so you can identify more accurately where you need to improve. You might be looking at the example I've given above and think, "That's great, but not all of my customers come from one source. How do I measure conversion rates when my customers come from lots of different places?"

This is a great question, and we'll come back to that after the following section. For now, though, I want to dig into how you can make sure your measurement activities are aligned with your marketing budget so that these two critical components are working together smoothly.

AN AGILE APPROACH TO SETTING YOUR MARKETING BUDGET

Traditionally, there are two approaches to budgeting:

1. Decide how much you can afford to spend and create a plan that fits that budget.
2. Decide what you want to achieve, create a plan that'll get you there and then cost it up.

The problem with the first approach is that it doesn't take into account your goals. Most business owners, when I ask them if they have a budget for marketing, say "Well, it depends on what I'm going to get back."

The problem with the second approach is that, too often, a business owner (or more commonly, the agency they've engaged) will get over-enthusiastic about their marketing, plan loads of expensive promotion activities and, after all the planning, realise that they can't fund the work. They're not prepared to get a loan or other investment to pay for it, because they're not confident it'll deliver.

I've seen this so often. It usually happens like this:

Agency: "Do you have a budget for your marketing?"
Business owner: "Not really."
Agency: "Then what are your goals for your marketing?"
Business owner: "I want to [take over the world in the next 12 months]."*
Agency: "OK then, we'll make a plan to do that."
Business owner: "Brilliant! I look forward to seeing it."

*Or some other over-ambitious goal on a small timescale.

These situations usually end with the business owner having a heart attack at the proposed cost of the marketing services.

This all changes when you're effectively measuring your marketing. You can see your conversion rates so you can effectively estimate how much you should get back in sales from any proposed marketing activity. This allows you to set a realistic budget that you feel confident working towards.

If you haven't started measuring your marketing yet, or if your marketing is currently minimal, so the data you have is inaccurate, setting a budget and creating a marketing plan can feel like a chicken-and-egg situation. How can you create a plan without knowing the budget, and how can you set a budget without knowing the plan? If that's where you're at, there's a third approach that will enable you to get started with your marketing planning before you know your conversion rates, and that's the Agile framework I mentioned earlier in the book.

If we use Agile principles, we can create a short-term, best-guess budget for the next quarter, which allows us to sidestep the chicken-and-egg scenario. Then as time goes on, we can test, iterate and use our measurement data to refine and improve.

Here's how to start:

1. Work out what you're currently spending and the results you're getting from that spend.

2. Decide whether you want to stick with that budget for the next 90 days or change it.
3. Create a plan to fit your budget and measure the results you get from your marketing.
4. In 90 days' time, review the results and reassess your budget.

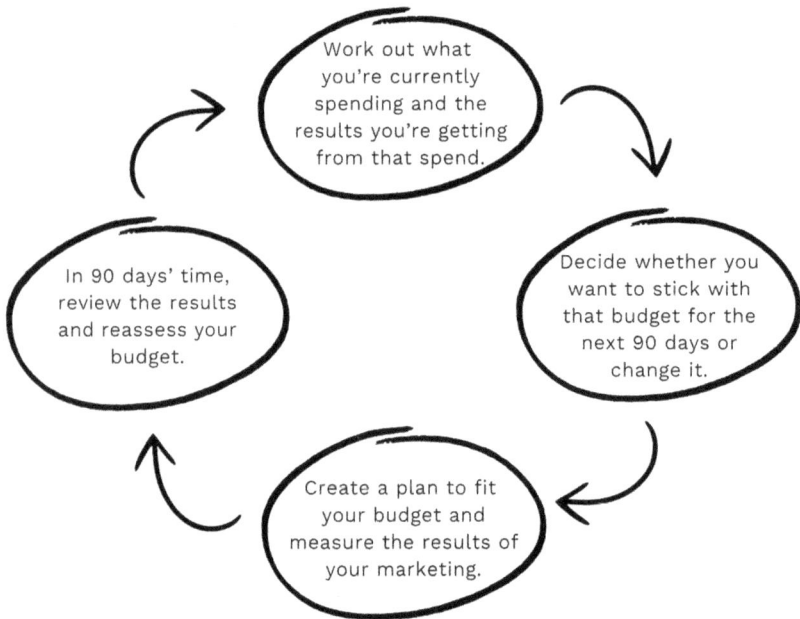

So let's get started.

First we need to know what resources you have available to acquire customers for your business.

Look at what you're currently spending on marketing. I find a spreadsheet is good for this, but a simple list works well too.

You need to include everything from regular monthly outgoings (such as your website hosting, PPC or email subscriptions, PR, or advertising) to other marketing costs like graphic design, printing, copywriting and web development that are more of a one-off. Make sure you include the costs of any networking you do and anything else that supports sales.

You should be able to find this number on your P&L if your accounts are in order.

Then work out how much time you or your staff spend on marketing activities. For example, how much time do your sales team spend on work-related social media? How much time do you spend going to networking events or sending press releases to newspapers? Add the salary costs for that time to your spreadsheet or list.

An alternative to this is to work out what marketing activity is done in-house and how much you'd expect to pay if you were to outsource this to a freelancer or agency.

Now consider how much you can afford to spend on marketing.

Many of the businesses I work with prefer to grow organically, rein-vesting their profits into generating sales instead of seeking investment.

Getting investment to spend on marketing can feel like a risk. However, once you're measuring effectively and can quantify the link between your sales results and your marketing efforts, it becomes much easier to confidently invest in marketing activities using a loan or outside invest-ment. Once you can see that every £1 you spend on marketing turns into, say, £2 of profit, why wouldn't you increase your marketing spend if you know you're going to get twice your money back in a few months' time?

If you're choosing to grow organically (meaning investing in growth without going into debt) then you'll need to know how much profit you have available to invest. This is where it's worthwhile speaking to your accountant or finance director, if you have one.

Another question to ask yourself is, how much would you comfortably commit to marketing if you were confident it would pay off?

I also ask my clients to set a time budget. How much time are they prepared to invest in their marketing? How many people do they have working on the marketing in their business, and how much time can each person commit to spending?

Some businesses have a small financial budget but make up for it by spending more time on their marketing. Others have very little time to spend on their marketing so they spend more money on it.

Don't overthink this. Remember, you're only setting your budget for the next three months. If, in three months' time, you decide that you set your budget too low or too high, you can change it. The point is to get you going with a sensible budget that will allow you to start capitalising on the opportunities within your current buyer journey — like getting them on to your "main road" from all the different routes they might be taking to find you. This brings us back to the question of how to measure customers coming to your business from different sources.

WHEN DO YOUR CUSTOMERS REACH THE "MAIN ROAD"?

Having mapped out your buyer journey, you've probably found that your "path to purchase" has many different entry routes. It should — you don't want to rely on only one channel when it comes to lead generation as it makes you vulnerable if that channel loses its effectiveness.

The problem that typically arises when you're measuring across your whole buyer journey is that it's not always easy to identify where the people came from originally. You might have 30 people clicking on your 'book a call' button every month, but did they come from your LinkedIn connections, your advert, a Google search, or from somewhere else?

Think of your buyer journey like a map of many different local roads leading to a main road. Your main road is where everyone ends up (often the company website), but sometimes the smaller roads don't converge until the point when people get in contact with you and the sales process starts. It varies from business to business, but it's important to know where your local roads meet the main road because that's where you're going to split your marketing metrics.

So we could describe the three parts of your marketing metrics as:

- The effectiveness of each of your local roads (the different sources customers are coming from).
- The effectiveness of your main road (your sales process or what happens after customers get in touch with you).
- How effectively you keep your customers in the car park once they've arrived (how frequently they buy from you).

PRACTICAL MEASUREMENT IN A SMALL BUSINESS

In engineering, there are usually rigorous quality assurance processes to make sure products are up to standard. But if you measured every single thing, you'd never get your product out the door. You can't always test every widget that comes off a manufacturing line or eradicate every single bug from a piece of software.

Instead, you take meaningful tests and measurements at regular intervals. You need to decide:

- When during the manufacturing process should you take samples to test?
- How often should you pull a sample from the line and test it?
- How will you effectively and efficiently test the sample to get useful results that will inform production and highlight any issues?

An engineer will always check the quality of a product's components and subassemblies as well as the product as a whole and, in the same way, we should measure the elements of our marketing as well as the whole marketing machine.

Measuring everything in a small business is usually completely unrealistic to begin with. It's the equivalent of wanting to get fit by running a marathon on the first day you ever go for a run. But marketing measurement doesn't have to be complex.

Here's how to do it...

HOW TO MEASURE LEAD GENERATION ACTIVITIES

The data you collect will, of course, depend on the marketing channels you use to generate leads, but the same principles apply to every channel.

Look at your buyer journey, then write down the points where you could measure the number of people passing through each marketing channel you use to generate leads. If you get confused, try imagining it as a road with junctions (points at which they can make a choice about where to go or what to do), and you want to count how many people pass through each junction. What would count as a junction?

To give you an example, if one of your lead generation channels is digital advertising, then people will pass the following junctions on their journey, and each of these has a metric associated with it:

- See the advert (reach).
- Click on the advert (clicks).
- Land on the website (new visitors on the landing page).
- Click on the 'call to action' button.

The next step will depend on your business. If the next action is to book a call with you, then you'll measure the number of clicks on your diary booking and possibly the number of actual bookings too. If the next step is to download your free guide, or sign up to your newsletter or buy a product then you'll measure that.

The goal is to keep your marketing measurement as simple as possible (to avoid overwhelm) while giving you the insights you need.

If you're currently in a position where all your leads come from referrals and word of mouth, then you may struggle to measure your lead generation, but don't give up. For now, you may just have to start measuring at the "main road" and that's fine. That's how I started, and how I start with a lot of clients.

HOW TO MEASURE LEAD NURTURING ACTIVITIES

Now that people have joined your main road, it's important to know how they're moving through the next part of the buyer journey and where you're losing potential customers.

In the buyer journey diagram, these are probably the people who are currently 'interested', 'considering', and/or 'buying in'.

You might already be measuring this as part of your sales process. Some business coaches refer to this as your "leads to quotes to sales" metrics, but I prefer to be more specific than that because what counts as a "lead" may be subjective. How are you qualifying them as a lead? We can minimise the subjectivity in our measurement processes by having unambiguous metrics that monitor people's behaviour rather than their characteristics. This might include:

- The number of first calls booked/taken.
- The number of first meetings booked/held.
- The number of proposals sent.
- The number of sales made to new customers.

Measuring these regularly will enable you to see your conversion rates at each stage of the buyer journey. Having a high proportion of potential customers moving successfully through each of these points in your buyer journey should indicate that your marketing is working effectively. A significant decrease in the number of leads between two of these points, however, indicates the point that you're losing potential customers and highlights where your current priorities are.

If you're a low-volume business that doesn't get (or need) a lot of new customers on a regular basis, then you may need to look at your data over a period of months or even years to get a useful conversion rate. I'll go into more detail about this when we look at how often to measure.

MAXIMISING CUSTOMER VALUE

As I said before, marketing isn't only about generating new leads for your business. It's also about nurturing your existing customers so they feel valued and confident buying from you again and again. This means your marketing measurement doesn't stop just because a customer has made a purchase.

Think of your marketing investment as "buying customers". My business is going to be much more profitable if I can buy valuable customers that make many purchases over many years. If most of my customers buy once and don't come back again, then I'm missing out on profit.

To identify more opportunities for maximising your average customer value, you might consider measuring:

- What is your average first purchase value? And what is your average subsequent purchase value?
- How many purchases do your customers make (on average) after their initial purchase, or for how long do customers typically keep coming back to you?
- How many active repeat customers do you currently have?
- How frequently do your customers buy from you?
- What percentage of your new leads have come from referrals from existing or past customers?

Having visibility on these metrics will also make you more confident in your lead generation investments because you may be able to work out which marketing activities generate the most valuable customers.

HOW OFTEN DO I MEASURE?

So that we're not wasting all our time measuring, we need to know how often to pull a sample from the production line or, in our case, some data from your marketing metrics.

If you measure too often you'll end up with too much data to be able to see any trends. Some days you'll get a flurry of leads and other days will be quiet, but that's nothing to worry about. On the other hand, you want to measure frequently enough so that an issue doesn't go unnoticed for too long and cause issues downstream.

Different businesses will need different frequencies when it comes to measurement and there's sometimes a bit of trial and error involved when it comes to getting it right. It's essential to have a rough understanding of how long a customer takes to travel the length of your buyer journey. If a customer typically buys within an hour of first hearing about you, then you could look at your conversion rates every day if you want to (and have time). On the other hand, if your customers often take weeks or months to make their buying decision then you'll get better data from measuring less often.

For example, if your customers typically take three months to decide whether to buy from you, there's no point taking measurements every day. For example, some days you might have more meetings than new enquiries, so your conversion rate (if checked daily) won't make sense. In this case, taking a measurement once a fortnight or once a month will provide a much clearer picture of your conversion rates.

There's also the issue of volume: if your business only needs one new customer a month to hit your goals, then you're unlikely to have enough traffic to give you useful data if you're measuring weekly. Some weeks you might have a few enquiries, zero first meetings, and one new customer, giving you very odd conversion rates.

Here at The Marketing Machine Works, we calculate our conversion rates monthly using a rolling three to six months of data. Businesses with low-volume, high-value sales may need to take the last year (or more) of data to get a useful conversion rate. Obviously this can be frustrating if you're making big improvements to your marketing as it will take time to see the changes in your conversion rates, but looking at your data on a regular basis using a fixed rolling period will show you emerging trends.

For us, it can be six months to a year (or more!) between first hearing about us and deciding to buy. People need to be in the right position to want marketing consultancy and sometimes they meet me when the timing isn't right. For many other businesses, it isn't so long. And I've worked with customers that have much longer buyer journey time spans than me.

ENSURING ROI

The most common question people ask me about measuring their marketing is: "Am I getting a return on investment from my marketing?"

This is a really important question to ask, but the problem is that most people assume that the only way to answer this question is to work out what your ROI is. I'm here to tell you, you don't need to know what your ROI is, you only need to know...

Is the money I'm spending on marketing generating profit? Yes or no?

These questions are subtly different because we're not trying to work out a complicated ratio of return on investment, we're just trying to find your "Go/No-Go" budget.

The Go/No-Go budget is the threshold we use to decide if your marketing investment is profitable enough to justify continuing (Go) or if it should be reassessed or stopped altogether (No-Go).

If you spend less than this threshold, you're in profit and making money: if you spend more, you're not. If you're spending a lot less than this number, you're really winning.

So how do we work out this number?

Well, by using your conversion rates to figure out how many people you can expect to move through your buyer journey, you can then work out how much you are willing to spend acquiring a long-term, loyal customer.

Imagine I have a "customer shop", and I'm selling happy, long-term, loyal customers. You can walk into my shop and buy a customer who you know is going to be worth whatever an average long-term customer is worth to your business.

How much are you prepared to spend buying that customer? The answer will, of course, depend on your business and I can't tell you what that number should be. It depends on how much it costs to deliver your product or service as well as your overheads like subscriptions, salaries, office space, admin, and so on.

For some businesses, they might be happy to spend £5 per customer while for others, it could be thousands. If you know what your profit margin is then that's a good place to start. A good accountant should be able to help, if you're completely stuck. Or you could do what a lot of my customers do when we first start working together, which is pick a number that feels about right and then refine it later!

However you do it, you need to be able to set yourself a budget so that, for an average customer, you'd be happy spending your budgeted amount acquiring them. We call that your customer acquisition cost.

Now we know how much we can afford to spend acquiring a new customer, we can use our conversion rates to work out how much we can spend on a marketing activity and still get ROI.

(Warning to maths-phobes: there's a bit of maths coming up, but this is as bad as it gets. Remember, if you find this section overwhelming or stressful, you can always take this information to a trusted financial colleague or advisor.)

Let's go back to the example of the buyer journey I used earlier...

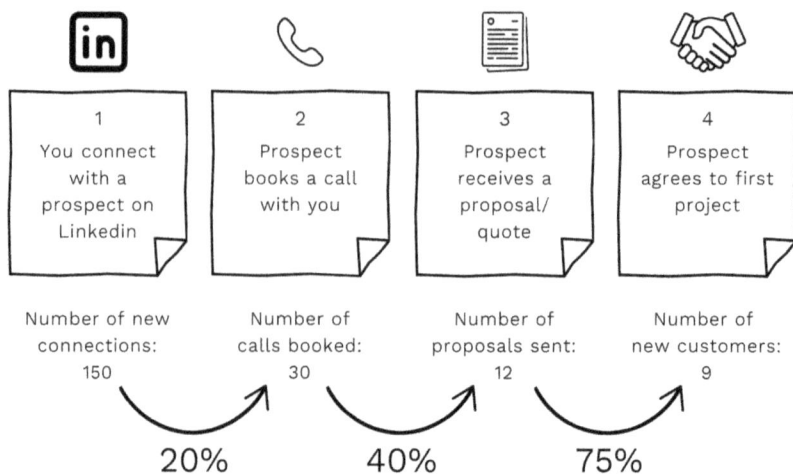

1	2	3	4
You connect with a prospect on Linkedin	Prospect books a call with you	Prospect receives a proposal/ quote	Prospect agrees to first project

| Number of new connections: 150 | Number of calls booked: 30 | Number of proposals sent: 12 | Number of new customers: 9 |

20%   40%   75%

In this example, let's say we're happy to spend £200 acquiring each customer. This means our total budget to acquire our nine customers is £1800. Now we can use our conversion rates to figure out how many people we could afford to 'buy' at each stage of the buyer journey.

Note that we are not spending chunks of our £200 budget at every stage of the buyer journey — at any one stage we could spend our *entire* £1800 across all prospects at that stage and still expect to see a total cost of £200 per customer acquired at the final stage of the journey.

So: if we are happy to spend £200 acquiring a new customer, and 75% of people who receive a proposal become a new customer, then how much can I spend getting someone to the point of requesting a proposal? The answer is I can spend $75\% \times £200$ (or $75 \times 200 \div 100$), which is £150 per person.

Now we know £150 per person is my budget to get someone up to the stage of requesting a proposal, but that's not all that useful because there aren't any marketing activities I can do that'll deliver me a prospect who has already received a proposal. So let's keep going — how much could we spend on getting people to book a call with us?

If we can spend £150 getting someone to request a proposal, and 40% of people who book a call request a proposal, then I could spend $40\% \times$

£150, or £60, getting people to book a call. This number is a bit more useful because there are marketing agencies who offer the service of finding prospects and getting calls booked. So if you were using a service like this, now you have a budget with which to hold them accountable. But not all businesses suit this kind of service, so let's keep going.

Continuing back through the buyer journey, we can now work out that we could spend £12 getting someone to connect with us on LinkedIn.

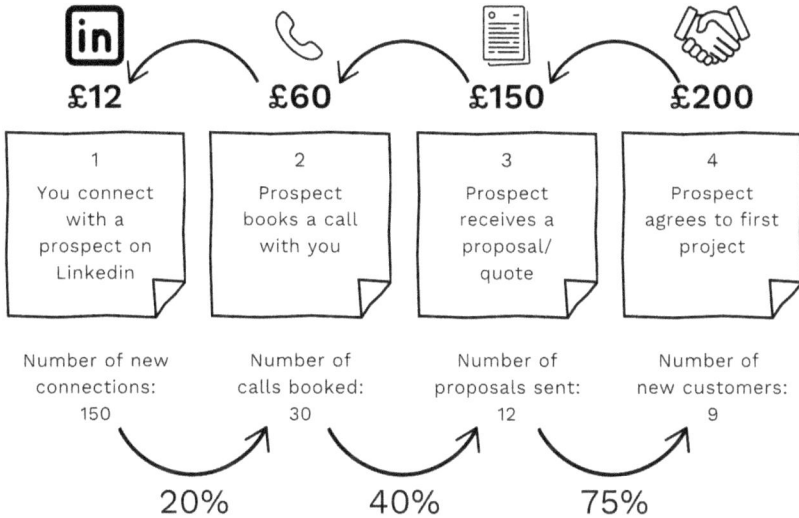

So using this data, we can now look at how much time it takes to find a prospect and connect with them on LinkedIn. If I also start measuring how many people I send connection requests to, I can work out the conversion rate from 'connections sent' to 'connections accepted'. Say this conversion rate was 30%, I now know I can spend £3.60 per connection sent out.

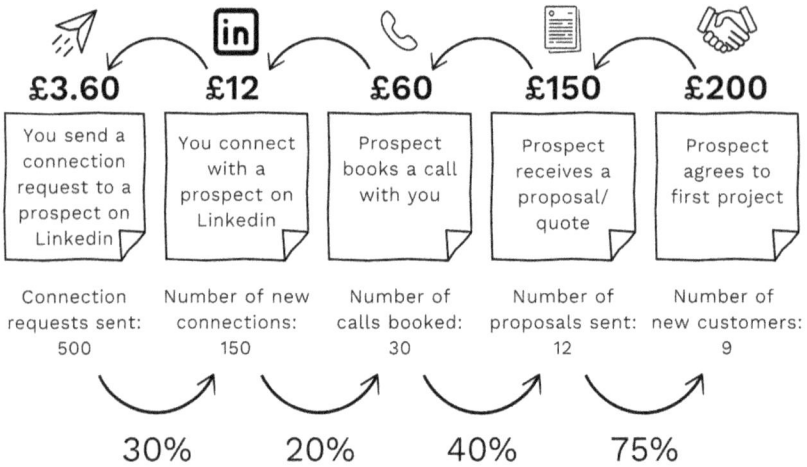

£3.60 — £12 — £60 — £150 — £200

You send a connection request to a prospect on LinkedIn	You connect with a prospect on LinkedIn	Prospect books a call with you	Prospect receives a proposal/ quote	Prospect agrees to first project

Connection requests sent: 500 — Number of new connections: 150 — Number of calls booked: 30 — Number of proposals sent: 12 — Number of new customers: 9

30%   20%   40%   75%

If it costs us £3.60 for every connection request we send out, and we do that 500 times for a total cost of £1800, assuming our conversion rates stay the same then those connection requests should convert into...

- 150 connections, which convert into...
- 30 calls booked, which convert into...
- 12 proposals sent out, which eventually convert into...
- Nine new customers.

Therefore those nine new customers cost us £1800 to acquire, which equates to £200 per customer.

This is where measurement gets really exciting. If this was your business and you were paying someone to send out connection requests on your behalf then this data enables you to keep them accountable. It means you can keep track of whether their effort is value for money for you. If you're using an agency to deliver leads, then you can qualify what that means to you and quantify how much that lead is worth.

This is also why it's so important to look for opportunities to increase your conversion rates at every stage of the buyer journey. If our conversion rates were higher then we'd be able to spend more on our lead generation. I'll explain exactly how to increase your conversion rates later when we look at improving your buyer journey, but for now let's take a look at what happens if we were to do this.

Let's imagine we can improve our marketing in such a way that we increase the conversion rate between connecting on LinkedIn and booking a call from 20% up to, say, 30%. With this new-and-improved conversion rate, instead of being limited to spending £12 getting the connection on LinkedIn, we'd be able to spend £18 getting that connection (£60 × 30%) and £5.40 sending a connection request (£18 × 30%, which is the existing conversion rate between connection requests sent and connections accepted).

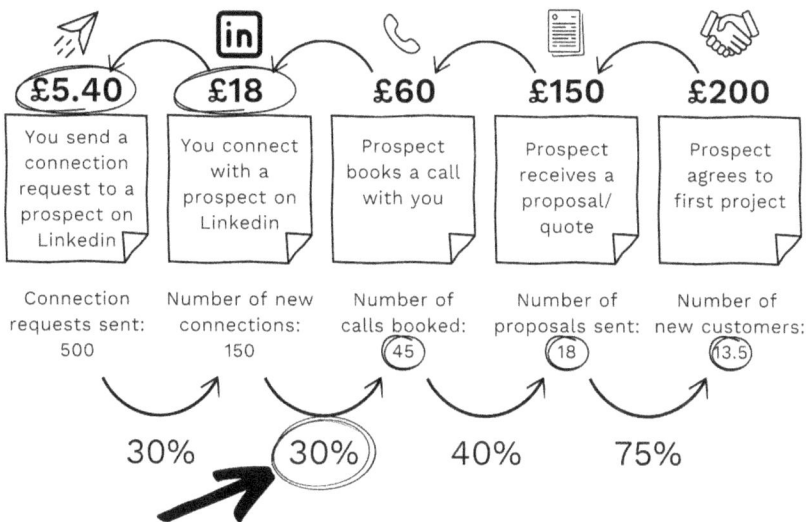

From a practical point of view this increase in budget would mean we can either spend a bit more time finding really good people to connect with and writing a personalised message to them, or we can make more profit.

Another exciting thing happens when we increase our conversion rate. We're still sending out the same 500 connection requests but, with our increased conversion rate, those connection requests are now converting into 13.5 customers (on average, that is — I'm not sure what half a customer looks like in real life) instead of nine customers. Again, you can now see how working on your marketing to improve your conversion rates makes a business much more profitable.

Tracking this kind of data over time, you can also see whether the person doing your marketing activities (an employee or external marketer) is maintaining a consistent conversion rate or whether their conversion rate is changing. If it's dropping, perhaps their targeting is becoming too broad or the channel is becoming less effective and other channels need to be considered instead. Keep an eye on your conversion rates and budget at each stage to make sure your marketing stays profitable.

Our example buyer journey above started with a LinkedIn connection but let's imagine a completely different buyer journey. In this one a Google advert leads to a website, followed by a shopping basket and an online checkout.

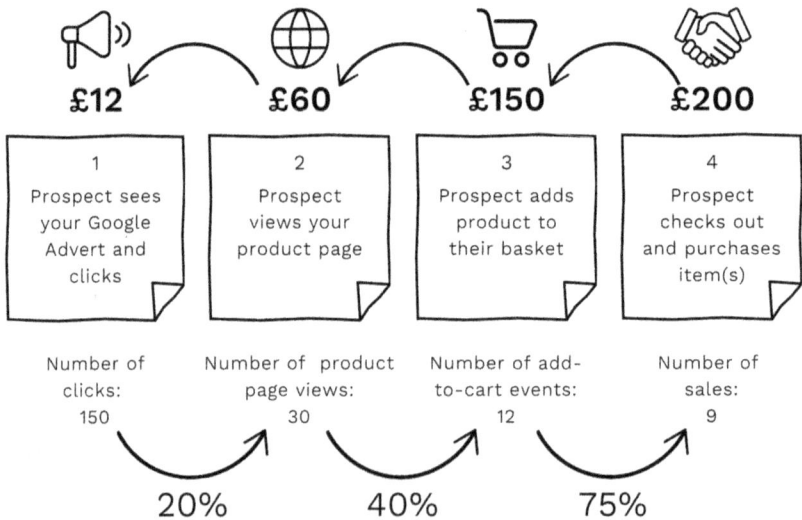

£12	£60	£150	£200
1	2	3	4
Prospect sees your Google Advert and clicks	Prospect views your product page	Prospect adds product to their basket	Prospect checks out and purchases item(s)
Number of clicks: 150	Number of product page views: 30	Number of add-to-cart events: 12	Number of sales: 9
	20%	40%	75%

For simplicity, and to save our calculators, let's imagine the conversion rates and customer acquisition cost are the same.

In this example, we can spend up to £12 per click on our digital advertising. That's such useful data!

If this was your business and you were spending less than £12 per click on your Google ad, then we'd be able to confidently say, "Yes, you're getting ROI. You're making money." If you were spending more than £12 per click then we could look at the rest of our buyer journey and see if we could improve our conversion rates somewhere. While we're making improvements we could pause our digital advertising so we don't waste money and switch them back on again when we've improved our marketing.

If you're starting a brand new marketing activity, you'll usually have to spend a bit of money up front "priming the engine". What I mean is you'll need to get a few people through the buyer journey (or a few stages into the journey) so you have some conversion rates to use to calculate if it's over or under your budget. This might seem like a waste, but it doesn't have to cost a lot of money because you only need to pay for enough people to go through the process to get reliable conversion rates. And it's a lot cheaper than spending money for months and months having no idea if it's generating any return on that investment. Gone are the days when you had to pay for 12 months of Google Ads before you could tell if they were working. Give it a month or so to get some data and then analyse what you get.

And just to show you how well this method can work in a small business, we received this email from one of our lovely clients, Electra Savvidou at Action PAs. She said...

> "I looked over my goals I set last year for marketing. In 12 months we wanted to...
>
> Raise our conversion rate from 30% to 36%... it's now 65%.
>
> Increase the average monthly spend per customer from £300 to £500... it's now £750.
>
> Get 20 retainer clients, which we have!
>
> We've tripled our business in a year."

So to sum up, the most important metrics you want to be measuring are...

1. How many people are at each stage of your buyer journey?
2. What are your conversion rates between each stage?
3. How much are you prepared to spend acquiring a new customer?

With measurement, it can be really tempting to jump in and try and measure everything, but this will just leave you feeling overwhelmed. As I said earlier, if you're new to measurement just pick three or four steps in your buyer journey like I've done in the examples, as this will give you enough information about a particular activity to see where there are opportunities to improve your conversion rates and whether your marketing is within your budget or not.

If you find you're really getting into measurement and want to take it further, you can start thinking about methods like A/B split testing, where (for example) two different versions of a web page might be created and visitors are shown one at random when they visit. A/B split testing is a great way to find out whether small tweaks like a different headline, image or page layout increases or decreases conversion rates. There are many other measurement and testing tools available, and new ones are coming out almost daily, so look online for the hottest new tools when you read this.

By incrementally improving your marketing, based on actual data, you'll save a fortune gambling your money on activities that you're not sure are working. You'll also be able to be more agile in your marketing as you'll be able to see and adapt when the market changes to stay ahead of your competitors. And if you're a marketing manager or marketing agency, these methods will enable you to confidently request more budget and quantifiably demonstrate how valuable your work is.

———

END OF CHAPTER CHECKLIST

I have:

☐ Identified where my "local roads" meet my "main road" and where I'm going to split my marketing measurement.

☐ Identified the key metrics I'm going to measure over the next quarter.

☐ Worked out my acceptable customer acquisition cost.

☐ Used my customer acquisition cost to work out my marketing budget for my lead generation activities (if doing lead generation).

☐ Decided how often to record my metrics and how often to review my conversion rates.

☐ Laid out an Agile marketing budget for the next quarter.

CHAPTER 8
OBJECTIVES

Metrics are the dashboard of your marketing machine. They give you the vital signs and signals you need to keep moving in the right direction. And they're the solid foundation you need for setting clear, measurable objectives.

Without reliable data, setting objectives is like firing arrows in the dark and hoping to hit the bullseye. By analysing the numbers, you can set goals that are realistic, focused, and tied directly to your broader business strategy. In this chapter, we'll turn the metrics from the last chapter into actionable objectives, ensuring your marketing efforts don't just drift — they deliver.

When I first started working in marketing, I hated setting objectives. I felt like I was setting myself up to fail if I planned a marketing activity that explicitly stated what it needed to achieve in order to be successful.

I also didn't understand that the first time you run a marketing activity, you have to make a lot of assumptions. Unless you've spent a fortune on customer research then your ideal customer, your proposition, and your buyer journey will all be full of assumptions. Some of them may turn out to be wrong, and that's a normal part of honing your marketing machine.

Think of your objectives like a scientific hypothesis for your marketing. We need to set clear, measurable goals that will guide our actions and allow us to evaluate and improve efficiently. Some of our marketing will involve experimentation, so let's be scientific about it.

No scientist worth their credentials will undertake a research project without a hypothesis, but this is what marketers do all the time when they say, "Let's put stuff out there and see what happens!"

A scientific hypothesis proposes an expected outcome of the experiment. In the same way, I want you to hypothesise what you expect or want to happen when you improve your marketing.

While scientists test their hypotheses using experiments to collect evidence, marketers test objectives through campaigns, along with strategies to track metrics and assess results. In both cases, the outcomes are measurable, and success (or failure) gives us insights we can use to refine our strategy and activities.

Objectives are a benchmark we can measure against.

I used to think of objectives as a stick to beat yourself up with. Now I know they're a tool to make your marketing more effective.

It's often tempting to sidestep this phase or start with a rough outline of what you want to achieve, but if you want your marketing to deliver results quickly and cost-efficiently then you need to make sure you've thought through the outcome.

There are two kinds of objectives: strategic objectives and tactical objectives.

Your strategic objectives look at the big picture of all your marketing, sales and after-sales processes. This is the hypothesis for what your whole marketing machine needs to deliver.

Your tactical objectives look at each individual marketing activity or campaign. These objectives are for all the components in your marketing machine, such as email campaigns, advertising campaigns or exhibitions.

But before we start with marketing objectives, we need to have business objectives.

BUSINESS OBJECTIVES

Your marketing objectives are what your marketing machine needs to deliver, but those objectives can only work if they're aligned with your business objectives — i.e., what your business needs to deliver.

If you already have clear business objectives, now's the time to dust them off and check them against the criteria we'll cover in this section. If your objectives are a little vague or only exist in your head (or the business owner's head), don't worry — read on, and we'll get them sorted.

I'm assuming you're the business owner or CEO and in a position to define these objectives yourself. If you're not, it's essential to have this conversation with whoever holds the reins, so your marketing objectives align seamlessly with the broader goals of the business. After all, a marketing machine running in a different direction from the business is like a car trying to drive with the wheels pointing different ways — it's not going to get very far.

All your objectives need to be SMART:

This stands for...

- Specific
- Measurable
- Achievable
- Relevant
- Time-bound

I should be able to ask you at a specified time in the future whether you've achieved this goal, and the answer can only be yes or no. There should not be any room for "it depends".

Take a few minutes now to think about specific business goals for what you want your business to achieve in the next three months, 12 months or whatever timescale you like to plan for.

Your business objectives are the high-level goals for the whole business. Often these goals include things like:

- Increase revenue (or turnover) by X%, or increase to £X.
- Increase profit margin from X% to Y%.
- Increase number of employees to X.

Depending on what's important to you as a business, and what you're already measuring, some businesses also like to set goals around customer satisfaction ratings, market share, product development, employee retention or sustainability.

To make sure these goals are realistic and achievable, we need to break them down into tangible, sense-checked outcomes that the business can work towards.

If your business objectives are to increase revenue, for example, then work out what that means in terms of sales. How many of each of your products or services do you plan to sell to achieve that revenue target? Is that realistic? Do you have the capacity and resources to deliver that number of products or sales? What would your business have to look and function like if you achieved this?

Look at what you've achieved in the past and think about your industry and the size of your market. Make sure your business objectives feel achievable to you and relevant to your overarching goals and vision.

It's often useful to model a few scenarios at this point. For example, if I wanted to achieve a goal of £2M turnover in the next 12 months, I might work out that I'd need to sell 700× Product A + 100× Product B + 10× Product C. I could also achieve the same goal by selling 300× Product A + 200× Product B + 30× Product C. ... Or I could sell another combination of products.

With each scenario, I can compare the target to our current sales levels, our production capacity (or delivery capacity if I'm selling services) and our profit margins to decide which scenario is (a) most achievable and (b) most profitable.

Consider how many of those sales you'll get from new customers and how many from existing customers. If you work in different markets then I recommend you break down the sales you plan to get from each market. This will show you which of your ideal customers you need to improve your marketing towards, which will affect your marketing objectives.

I highly recommend using a spreadsheet for this kind of analysis and, if you don't have a financial director in your business, it may be useful to do this with a good accountant or fractional CFO by your side.

Years ago, I did this exercise for my consulting and training business and discovered that the goal turnover I'd set for myself meant that I'd be working far more hours than I was able to, given the childcare commitments I had at the time. I had set a revenue goal, but when I worked out how many training courses and consultancy days I'd need to deliver to meet that goal, I realised I didn't have enough hours in my (then part-time) week to achieve it. I knew I didn't want to work evenings and weekends as well, so I had to start looking differently at my business model, the services I offered and my profit margins on each service.

I used a spreadsheet to look at what would happen if I increased or decreased the number of training courses I delivered compared to consultancy time and what the result would be in terms of hours worked and profit. It felt arduous at the time, because I'd never looked in detail at all the costs of the different courses and consultancy engagements I delivered. I also had to keep sense-checking my results to make sure that the goals I was setting were realistic given the position I was starting from. But I ended up with a much more profitable business as a result.

Some objectives, like market share, can be harder to measure as a small business, which is why I tend to avoid objectives like this. If you're setting sustainability goals or customer satisfaction goals, for example, it's essential to be able to measure them so make sure you've considered your metrics on these fronts too.

Write down your business objectives and sales breakdown (if relevant to your goals) in your notebook or Marketing Machine Journal.

STRATEGIC MARKETING OBJECTIVES

Once you've set your business objectives, we then need to create marketing objectives that will support them.

This is where your metrics come in.

You've mapped out your buyer journey and you understand how conversion rates work (and perhaps you've already started measuring them too!), so it's time to think about what you need your marketing to achieve. Look at your buyer journey and decide where you're going to focus your marketing efforts.

Is your best bet to increase the number of people starting your buyer journey (lead generation)?

Perhaps your conversion rates from enquiry to sale are lower than you'd like, so focusing on the middle of the buyer journey (lead nurturing) makes more sense?

Or maybe you're leaving money on the table when it comes to selling more to existing customers, and increasing customer value should be your priority?

I won't get into how to tackle each of these objectives right here because the approach you'll take will vary wildly depending on where you're trying to make an impact. We also need to make sure we know what resources we have to play with before we start planning our marketing activities — the budget we talked about earlier, and the personnel, which we'll discuss in the 'Prioritise, Plan, Propel' chapter. First, pinpoint the part of your buyer journey that needs the most attention. Then, you'll be ready to explore the 'how' later in a way that fits your business perfectly.

If you're already measuring your conversion rates, you might have started to notice places where you're losing customers along the buyer journey. If your business objectives are to increase turnover by, say, 20%, then your marketing objectives might be to increase your conversion rate from enquiry to proposal by 20%. If we know that our current conversion rate is 40% then our goal conversion rate will be 48% — a

20% increase. If we have 20% more people converting from enquiry to proposal then our sales should likewise increase by 20%.

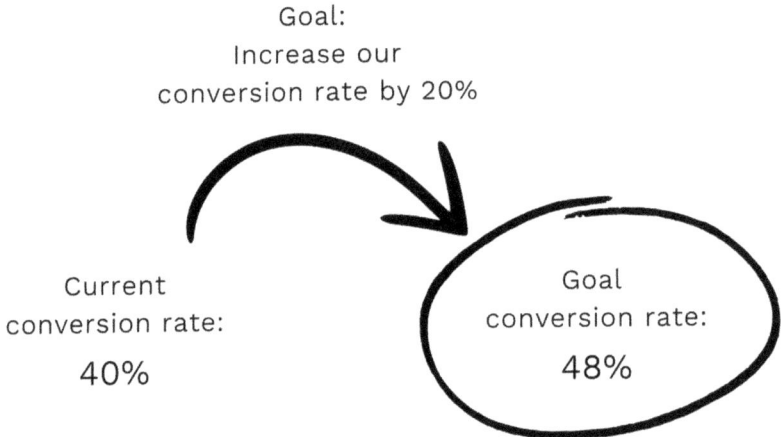

Goal:
Increase our
conversion rate by 20%

Current
conversion rate:
40%

Goal
conversion rate:
48%

You could also achieve the same objective by increasing sales to existing customers by 20% or increasing new enquiries by 20%.

If you're a small business with limited resources then you may decide that one of these goals is enough. Larger businesses might decide to tackle more than one area of the buyer journey at a time, and set objectives such as:

- Increase sales to existing customers by 5%.
- Increase conversions of qualified warm leads into customers by 5%.
- Increase new enquiries by 10%.

Because we're talking about percentages of percentages, these three objectives will result in a 17.7% increase in sales. There's a spreadsheet template for you to use on my website where you can input your own numbers and work out the best objectives to meet your goals.[1]

If you're measuring your marketing already, look at your conversion

---

1. https://rosconkie.com/TheMarketingMachineResources

rates and specify what you want your conversion rates to increase from and to.

If you're not measuring yet, it's worth estimating what you think (or hope!) your metrics and conversions are and then building on that. Even just looking at how many enquiries you had in the last month, how many calls or meetings with new customers you took, and how many sales you won, can give you a useful starting point to set objectives from.

Again, check that your marketing objectives are realistic and achievable given your industry, market size and resources. Check they will achieve your business objectives by thinking about the length of time it takes for your customers to complete their buyer journey. If your customers typically take six to 12 months to buy from you, then setting marketing objectives around generating more awareness will not lead to any more sales within three months. That might be fine if your business objectives are long-term and you don't need an immediate sales injection, but if your quarterly business objectives include a sales increase then you need to consider where those sales will come from.

Write down your strategic marketing objectives in your notebook or Marketing Machine Journal.

TACTICAL OBJECTIVES

Your tactics are the components of your marketing machine that support your customers on their buyer journey. In other words, all your marketing activities. So your tactical objectives are your hypotheses for the results you expect from your individual marketing tactics.

Like all the other objectives, we need our tactical objectives to be SMART (Specific, Measurable, Achievable, Relevant and Time-bound).

First, be specific. What do you want to achieve with this marketing activity? Which strategic objective is it supporting?

What is the end result you are hoping for? The purpose of every piece of marketing is to help people move forward in their decision-making process, so where in your buyer journey is this activity acting and what is the next stage it needs to point towards? How will you measure the conversion rate of this activity? Plan your metrics as part of your objective-setting process.

Again, make sure your objectives are achievable given the resources available and relevant to your strategic and business objectives. Setting a tactical objective of posting on Instagram four times a week without any regard for how that will achieve your strategic and business objectives will likely turn out to be a waste of time. And take a moment before setting your objective to do a quick sanity check: don't set yourself a tactical objective of creating a new lead generation campaign, for example, if your strategic objective is to increase revenue from existing customers.

Tactical objectives might include ongoing activities, such as posting on LinkedIn twice a week and publishing a new blog once a month. They may also include one-off activities, such as sending a direct-mail campaign to 200 people who fit specific criteria that mean they could be an ideal customer.

You might even set a tactical objective that focuses on a conversion rate instead of the output. For example, implement an A/B split test on copy, call to action and layout of your landing page to increase conversion by 5%. If your strategic marketing objective was to increase enquiries by 5% then this would be an excellent tactical objective.

It can take a bit of experience to set effective tactical objectives but the next few chapters will explain what you need to know to be able to make a good start. You may also want to revisit this section once you've set your marketing priorities to make sure each of those activities have an objective.

CHECKING YOUR BUDGET FITS YOUR OBJECTIVES

It's important to be constantly assessing the money you're spending on marketing against your objectives. This is a conversation to have with your finance director if you have one.

If you've set yourself a sales or revenue objective, It's time to check your objective against your marketing budget. Remember in the 'Measure and Test' chapter when we imagined "buying customers"? Now we are going to check how much we would expect to spend on marketing to buy the number of customers we want for our objectives.

So, for example, if you set yourself a sales objective of 100 new customers in the next three months, and you're happy to spend £100 buying each new customer, then your marketing budget will be £10,000 for the next quarter.

When you're doing this, remember that the "buying customers" exercise was for brand new customers, not existing customers. Hopefully you've broken your objective into 'sales from existing customers' and 'sales from new customers' so your marketing budget will be mainly focused on getting sales from new customers.

If you don't have a financial director in your business then this is where you may want to get some help from an advisor or fractional CFO to look at the implications and affordability of your budget.

The reason I keep coming back to the importance of measurement is because if you are confident in your conversion rates, you can be confident investing larger budgets in marketing.

———

END OF CHAPTER CHECKLIST

I have:

☐ Set my business objectives.

☐ Set my strategic marketing objectives.

☐ Sanity-checked my marketing objectives to check they support my business objectives.

☐ Cross-checked my budget with my objectives.

CHAPTER 9
OPTIMISING YOUR BUYER JOURNEY

As I've said throughout this book, marketing is all about making it really easy for people to buy from you. This is why your buyer journey is so important. Ideally, we want the path to purchase — from when your customer goes from not knowing anything about you to being a "raving fan" — to be as effortless and comfortable as possible.

In this chapter we're going to go through all the ways you can improve your buyer journey and make it even easier for people to buy from you. The companies that do this really well are a joy to buy from. Have you ever bought something and the whole process was so easy you just felt delighted? Companies like Amazon spring to mind for me. They're not my favourite company when it comes to values, but no one can deny they are exceptional at making it easy to purchase. Too easy, on occasion! Their buyer journey is utterly seamless and it makes it almost inevitable that customers will return to them over and over again because it's just so easy.

You've already mapped out your current buyer journey, so you've established the activities you currently have in place to support customers in their decision-making. That's not necessarily about speeding people up in their decision-making, though. Naturally, if it's easy for people to buy then they'll tend to get there quicker, but that's not the goal.

When customers aren't given enough time to fully consider their options, and they're rushed into a buying decision, they are much more likely to suffer "buyer's remorse" — that dreadful feeling of regret that comes after a bad buying decision. Buyer's remorse is expensive for a company. Operations have to deal with product returns, customer service is burdened with complaints and refunds, contracts become unprofitable when the customer drains your time and resources, and cash flow is screwed up when a customer refuses to pay their invoice. Believe me, it's much better to let your customer take their time deciding to buy, because when a customer is confident in their decision, they're likely to be much more profitable in the long-term.

Your marketing needs to pace people — to meet them where they are and help them move forward at a speed they're comfortable with. If your business is very relational, such as consultancy, training, coaching or therapy, you may also want to slow people down to make sure you're a good fit and that the outcome will be positive for both of you. There's nothing worse than saying yes to a customer who's desperate to buy quickly, and then finding out they're a nightmare to work with.

Looking at your buyer journey, you may notice that it probably has three sections to it:

1. Promotion and lead generation: this is the section from the start of the journey (when people hear about you for the first time) up until your customer makes contact with you for the first time. This is what most people think of as marketing.
2. Nurturing and closing: this is where your customers are seriously considering your product or service and comparing it with other options. Unless your business is entirely e-commerce, your sales team (or you, if you're a very small business) will likely get involved in helping your customers buy. Your marketing should support this sales activity.
3. Post-purchase support: this is often considered to be the responsibility of Customer Service or Account Management

but, as you'll see, there's a lot your marketing can do to increase customer satisfaction and encourage loyalty, repeat purchases and referrals.

I'm now going to walk you through a buyer journey showing you ways to optimise your marketing and make it easier for people to buy. At each stage I'll explain what your marketing needs to achieve to support your buyers as effectively as possible.

Since buyer journeys vary in length, I'm going to go through a long one (which means that this chapter is quite long and detailed). If your buyer journey is quite short then some of these tools and suggestions may not be appropriate or necessary for your business. If that's the case, or you feel like you're not ready for a particular section, move on.

If you realise you have nothing at all supporting your customers at a particular stage, don't panic! The goal with your marketing is to support the most risk-averse buyers. If you're already making money with the marketing you've got at the moment, then identifying an issue won't change that. It may be that the people who are buying from you are comfortable with a level of risk and so they don't need as much support. If you can add more support into your buyer journey, and nurture people who are very risk-averse through their decision-making, then you'll dramatically increase your sales.

Whenever you think of something you could do to better support your buyers, jot it down on a red post-it and add it to your buyer journey map. But don't jump into action just yet! Remember, we need to prioritise before implementing. This step is all about creating a marketing wishlist. Once your wishlist is complete, we'll move on to prioritising.

1. GETTING YOUR BUYER FROM 'UNAWARE' TO 'AWARE'

At the very start of your buyer journey, when your buyer is unaware you exist, your task is just to get on their radar. More specifically, you want to get on the radar of your ideal customer and people like them.

There are two things to think about here:

1. Where are they likely to hang out? In other words, where might they stumble upon your message if you showed up there?
2. Where might they look if they were actively seeking out what you offer?

Some businesses sell specific answers to problems and their customers seek them out by searching on Google, YouTube or other online platforms. For other businesses, the problem they solve isn't always obvious to the customer. I've worked with many businesses where we know it's pointless optimising for search because people simply aren't looking for them. In those cases, we have to show up where their customers are and disrupt them.

Most businesses want to be in a number of places and often a mixture of the two types I mentioned above. You definitely don't want to have all your eggs in one basket by only having one source of traffic to your business. It always makes me feel on edge when I see a business wholly reliant on digital advertising like Google Ads for their traffic. This may generate a lot of income for the business, but it also makes the business vulnerable to changes in the platform's algorithms. The same goes for a business where all your customers come from search engines, networking, a specific exhibition, or any other single activity. If that channel suddenly decided to change their rules, or if it folded entirely, what would happen to your business? The Covid-19 pandemic was a painful reminder of this when exhibitions were all cancelled and in-person networking ended. Companies that relied on these channels struggled to adjust.

There's another reason why it's important to promote across a number of channels and, again, it's all about perceived risk and trust. When we see something for the first time, we may notice it but our inner skeptic will be asking whether it's legitimate. If we see a brand everywhere, then that ubiquity breeds familiarity and trust. "No one gets fired for buying IBM", as the saying goes. For a small business, being "everywhere" is usually unaffordable, but it may be possible to be in a number of places that your ideal customer will see you. The more frequently they see you in different contexts, the more their unconscious mind will become familiar with you, which will build trust and reduce perceived risk.

If you're only promoting yourself in one place then you'll only attract those risk-takers who don't need to build up as much trust to make a decision. Anyone who needs to feel more familiar with a company or brand may not trust you enough to take action and you'll miss out on a big chunk of your market.

What this means for your marketing is that you need customers to hear about you from more than one different source, and preferably at least three. So, for example, you might undertake the following awareness-generating activities:

1. Advertise regularly in a publication your audience often reads.
2. Attend an exhibition that your audience attends.
3. Make sure you rank highly for the search terms your buyers typically use.

Of course, there's always an exception to a rule like this and that is "word of mouth".

As a channel, word of mouth works a bit differently because recommendations from three different people may count as three different sources (from the buyer's perspective).

More risk-taking buyers may be happy to ask only one person for a recommendation, while more risk-averse buyers will probably ask a few people and will only consider the options that have been recommended several times.

This is most apparent in my own buying behaviour when I'm looking for a tradesperson. I might post in my local Facebook group, "Does anyone know a good plumber in Portishead?" I'll then call the plumbers who have been mentioned most often in the comments.

If word of mouth recommendation is a big business generator for you then you need to make sure you stay front of mind with the people who are most likely to be asked for recommendations for your products or services. Go back to your ideal customer persona and look at the influencers you identified. If your customer is likely to ask specific people for recommendations then your marketing needs to include proactive networking with those influencers.

A client of mine is a mortgage advisor and is often recommended by local estate agents and solicitors. She makes sure she meets up regularly with these influencers so that she is front of mind when they're asked for a recommendation. In the same way, I make sure I network with people like business coaches, sales trainers, accountants and HR professionals, because these people often work with growing small businesses and, when the topic of marketing comes up I want them to think of me.

Each time someone sees you and your message, you'll build a little more trust with them. It can take time to build up that trust so, if you're doing a marketing activity like advertising, you may need to run your adverts for a while before evaluating their results. The more times someone sees your advert, the more familiar they'll become with your company and the more likely they'll be to respond to it. Google and Facebook know this: this is why digital adverts are usually shown to people more than once.

Awareness-generating activities you might consider

If you're short of ideas for awareness-generating activities, here's my checklist to get your juices flowing. Consider your ideal customer and which activities are most likely to be effective in getting your message in front of them at the moment when they're looking.

It's important to point out here that a common reason awareness-driving activities fail is not because the campaigns themselves are badly executed (although that is sometimes the case), but often because the next step in the buyer journey was not thought through. For example, it might look like a Google Ads campaign failed because it didn't generate any leads, but that may have been because when people clicked on the ad, the website didn't then do a good job of converting them into leads.

So before you dive into any of the activities below, make sure your whole buyer journey is clearly mapped out to incorporate this new activity and your next steps are clearly signposted and converting effectively.

If any of these activities sound like something that would work well for you, add them as a red post-it on your buyer journey and we'll figure out how high a priority they are when we come to prioritise in the next chapter.

- **Print advertising:** industry journals, magazines, newspapers, local newsletters, and printed billboards.
- **Digital advertising:** social media, digital advertising networks like Google AdSense, online directories, TV and radio, and digital billboards and signage.
- **Search advertising:** this is mostly Google Ads. I've listed this separately to digital advertising because the strategy and targeting are quite different. With digital advertising you're trying to get your message in front of someone when they're generally browsing the Internet. With search advertising you're trying to get people to click your ad when they are actively searching for something specific to your product or service.
- **Organic search marketing:** usually called search engine optimisation, or SEO.
- **Organic social media marketing:** creating shareable content such as videos, quizzes, memes, blogs, competitions etc., using appropriate hashtags and sharing useful content in groups.
- **Outbound social media approach:** finding prospects and connecting with them on social media such as LinkedIn, and then sending them a message offering some valuable content. Please don't set up an automated outbound marketing campaign with a message that tells the unsuspecting recipient all about how great your company is! Treat it in the same way you'd treat face-to-face networking — by starting a conversation, finding out if they may be interested in what you offer and then talking about what they might need.
- **Direct mailing:** this doesn't just have to be email (which is usually the lowest converting type of direct mailing). Consider

targeted postal mailings as well as door-drops if your business is very local.

- **Public Relations (PR):** this is a huge area of marketing that includes a wide variety of publicity for your business. It could include getting featured in an article in the press, winning an award, running a competition, hosting or sponsoring an event, holding an open day, or publicising some pro-bono or charity fundraising work you may be doing as a business.
- **Partnerships:** if you know of other businesses that are complementary and non-competitive to you, collaborations and partnerships can be valuable marketing opportunities. Consider whether you can each include a flyer of the other business's product or service with every order, or cross-promote by guest blogging.
- **Networking:** either at general business networking events or at specific industry conferences and exhibitions.
- **Cold calling or telemarketing/telesales**: this has a bad reputation but, done well, it can be very effective. The key is to assume the recipient is busy and not thinking about buying whatever you offer right now. With this mindset, your goal is only to find out whether they may be interested at some point, and we'll talk about this later in this chapter, in the section on supporting your customers at the consideration stage.
- **Exhibiting at shows or festivals**
- **Promoting and selling via distributors, agents, affiliates or licensees**

This list isn't exhaustive as new techniques are appearing all the time. I'm not going to go into detail about each of the activities above, since each one warrants a book by itself, and many of those books have already been written.

Keep in mind that the effectiveness of different techniques change over time. For example, as I write, social media advertising is waning in effectiveness for some industries because it's been overused by scammers and low-quality suppliers, and this makes consumers more risk-averse. Additionally, new tools are emerging with increasing rapidity. As I write, AI tools like ChatGPT and Google Gemini don't have advertising alongside their responses but I'm sure those companies are working on monetising these tools, which could potentially be an effective channel for many businesses.

When considering different awareness-generating tools, remember to consider that many of the above activities can be much more successful when used in combination. Here's an example of an effective combination for a business looking to work with a small number of specific customers:

1. The business owner or salesperson connects with 200 people on LinkedIn who are likely to be close to the ideal customer persona. The message is non-salesy and friendly.
2. A few days later, the potential customers receive a targeted direct mailing with a personalised letter and a valuable piece of content.
3. Another few days later, they receive a second message on LinkedIn asking if they received the content and whether it was useful. Depending on the audience, one or two more follow-up messages may be sent.
4. Anyone who has responded to any of the messages receives a phone call from the sales team (or business owner) to talk about the content sent and answer any questions. If they're interested, a video call or meeting is arranged.

The effectiveness of different strategies may change over time, especially when it comes to social media and digital advertising, so I recommend speaking to an experienced professional if you are considering adding any of these marketing activities into your buyer journey.

2. BUILDING BUYER'S INTEREST

Continuing along your buyer journey, your customer is now aware of you. Now your marketing needs to get your customer to really sit up and take notice.

Remember when we talked about your ideal customer, your proposition and your messaging? This is where you need to use all the "away from" and "towards" messaging you identified.

Think about your buyer's "Chimp Brain", and the headlines and subheadings that will wake up the Chimp and then immediately reassure them they're in the right place to solve that problem.

If you're writing a headline for a landing page, bear in mind how people got to that page in the first place. It may be that your advert needs to have the "away from" and the landing page has the "towards" messaging. If you're creating a landing page that will come after a specific digital advert, make sure the problem you're talking about on the landing page is the same one that your advert headline highlights.

Now you have your buyer's attention, you need to let them get to know you in *their* own time. As I said, marketing is not about speeding people up in their decision-making, it's about making it easy for people to buy from you. If it's really easy to buy then people may well naturally speed up a bit, but that is a by-product of good marketing and not the objective.

To build your buyer's interest, your marketing needs to establish trust and authority by providing regular, high-quality, short-form content. You may have heard the phrase "content marketing" before — this is where it comes into play in your buyer journey.

What is content marketing?

"Content marketing" means sharing genuinely useful, relevant content that draws your ideal customers to you. This might be blog posts, videos, podcasts, social media updates, white papers or whatever type of content feels like a fit for your business. The purpose of this is simple: to enable your ideal customers to get to know and trust you before they buy.

Businesses didn't need content marketing just a couple of decades ago, but almost all businesses do now — so what's changed? To explain the purpose of content marketing, first I need to explain how buyer behaviour has changed.

As consumers we are all changing our behaviour due to the vast amounts of information we have at our disposal. Over the 20 years I've worked in marketing, there has been a lot of research into how buyer behaviour has changed, and personally I've noticed a significant change in buyer behaviour.

How did we buy before the Internet?

1. We walked into a shop and talked to a sales assistant.
2. We looked in the Yellow Pages and phoned 10 companies asking them all to send us a brochure.
3. We asked someone we knew who had previously bought this product or service who they used.

We still ask trusted contacts for advice, but we'll probably still do our own research before we go ahead with a purchase. Most of us certainly aren't combing through directories and requesting pamphlets!

So how do we buy now?

1. We check out products online, and read reviews and articles before we go to a shop or make contact with a supplier.
2. We have much less interaction with sales assistants when we go into a shop, since we expect to have most of our questions answered through our pre-shop research.
3. For straightforward, transactional purchases, we expect to be able to do the whole thing quickly and efficiently, without any human interaction or conversation.
4. We Google people before we go on a first date... oh wait, that's not related to marketing! (All the same, I suspect it's the same trend manifesting in a different context.)

What these examples have in common is that people are much further on in their decision-making process when they make contact with the seller (or potential life partner). They've educated themselves and weighed up the options before making themselves known to the shop or supplier.

I believe there are two reasons for this:

1. We expect to be able to make informed decisions.

There is so much information available at our fingertips (literally, via our phones), we expect to be able to learn much more about what we buy before we approach the seller. We'll look at website product descriptions, online reviews, video demonstrations and so on. These things all help us learn almost everything we need to know about a product or service without any conversation with the seller. And, as consumers, we have come to expect these resources to be available.

Before the Internet, if we bought something that turned out to be rubbish, we knew there wasn't much we could've done to avoid it. We did our best but there was no way we could've reduced the risk of buying. Now, because there is so much information available online, we can more effectively weigh up the risk of buying. We can look at how many one-star reviews there are compared to the five-star reviews. We can decide for ourselves how much risk there is and whether we're comfortable taking that risk.

2. We are much more cautious about giving our data to companies we don't know.

Many (perhaps most) of us have, at some point, given away our data only to end up being spammed or contacted incessantly by someone. For years I got phone calls from a double-glazing company after I made the mistake of clicking "request a quote" on their website. We've all fallen foul of the over-zealous automated email sequence. Nowadays it's easy for companies to set up marketing automations and too many of them forget to stop and think about whether it's what their buyers actually want. As a result, we're all now very hesitant to hand over our data until we are sure we trust the sender. This also means we are typically much further along in our decision-making process before we make contact with a seller.

Our marketing needs to recognise these two needs:

1. We need to empower our buyers to make informed decisions, using

content marketing to inform and build confidence in our products and services.

2. We need to respect our buyers' data by complying with GDPR (not to mention common courtesy) and only collect the data we really, absolutely need. Any more and it'll put buyers off.

How do we use content marketing to help buyers make informed decisions?

In a nutshell, you need to have much more information readily available to your customers than you would have 20 years ago. For most businesses this means having a much more informative website.

Your marketing needs to help your customers build a relationship with you, so think of the content at the beginning of your buyer journey as the "first date" in your relationship. It needs to be content that buyers can access quickly and find immediately valuable. Use it to demonstrate your credibility and help your buyers educate themselves in your area of expertise. Because content marketing is all about education and trust-building, it supports our most risk-averse buyers who need to deeply understand and trust something before they're happy buying.

Most people start content marketing by adding short blog articles to their website. This is a great place to start especially if people buy from you because of your expertise. If you're more comfortable speaking than writing, start by making short videos instead. If you transcribe them into a blog afterwards you'll have two pieces of content in one hit! I have a few clients who dictate their ideas into a document, as if they're talking to a customer or friend, and then tidy it up into a blog.

If you're not sure what to talk about, go back to the Ideal Customer chapter where I talked about how to draw out content ideas from your ideal customer persona.

When you're in a good rhythm of content creation, branch out into other types of content. Ideally, you want to build up a wide range of different types of content, but add one at a time to avoid overwhelm.

Here are some types of content marketing you can create to help people get to know you before they buy:

- Social media posts
- Blogs and short articles
- Short videos
- Podcasts
- Infographics
- Presentations (record a video of yourself presenting it using a tool like Zoom or Loom, or export it as a video or PDF deck if your slides are self-explanatory)
- Animations
- Quizzes
- Short templates
- Useful tools such as a ROI calculator or comparison tool

It's important to use a variety of different types of content, because we all have different preferences when it comes to learning. Some of us prefer to read, some to watch and some to listen. Recycle your content into different formats so it is accessible to people with different preferences.

For example, if you have a presentation with five key points in it, each of those points could be written out as a blog with a couple of accompanying social media posts or short videos. The five points could be illustrated in an infographic, or animation. You could even create a quiz to help people identify which of the five points they're struggling with. This one idea has given you a presentation, five blogs, 10 social media posts, 10 videos, an infographic and a quiz: up to 28 pieces of content!

These pieces of content need to demonstrate your knowledge, authority and experience to build trust and help buyers educate themselves in how to make their decision.

What should I talk about in my content?

I get asked this a lot, and it's an important question. You don't want to waste your time creating content that no one consumes. Plan your topics to make sure they're interesting and valuable to your ideal customer, so keep this person in your mind when you're creating content.

I've already talked about how to pull ideas out of your ideal customer persona, but here are a few more ideas for content topics:

- Tips: what nuggets of advice can you give your customer?
- FAQs: what questions or concerns might they have about your product or industry?
- Insights, trends and topical issues: what's going on in your industry at the moment?
- Opinion pieces/commentary: offer your expert opinion on timely industry news.
- Success stories, case studies and key learnings from projects you've worked on: readers can see how other people have benefitted from your work.
- Best practice advice: advising readers on how to tackle common scenarios your business supports.
- Relevant research and statistics: interpret the data and help readers make sense of the numbers.
- Common misconceptions: bust those myths!

Keep going back to your ideal customer persona for inspiration.

A lot of the best ideas for short (or "short-form") pieces of content come from the questions your customers most commonly ask you, common misconceptions about your industry, or concerns and issues that arise when buying. Refer back to your ideal customer persona, in particular their attitudes and beliefs, and see if you can create some content around those areas.

The best thing about short-form content is its versatility. Once you've created it, there are loads of ways you can use it to support people at different stages of their buyer journey. You could...

- Create a digital advert that directs people to a blog on a commonly searched question.

- Link to the content on social media when people are discussing the topic.
- Send a prospective customer a link to the content when they ask the question.
- Create a newsletter on the same topic and email it to your existing customers.
- If someone asks a question in a social media group that you have content on, write a short summary answer and then link to your content for them to read the more in-depth answer.
- Rewrite a popular blog article and send it to someone who may want to use it as a guest blog on their site, or send it to a relevant publication as PR.
- Research which phrases and questions your audience often search for and create or repurpose content that answers one of these questions. This will help people find you when they are searching.

The importance of the Call to Action (CTA)

As I've said, the aim of marketing is to support customers through their buying journey. This means every single piece of marketing — including every piece of marketing content — should have a call to action that leads your customers on to the next step.

Crafting an effective call to action is easier said than done. Here are two things to keep in mind:

1. Decide on the best "next step" in the buyer journey.

Does it make sense for customers to go there next? Make sure it's an easy step along the buyer journey for them to take without feeling like it's risky. Sometimes it can be helpful to offer more than one next step (just be careful not to offer too many choices, as that can confuse or overwhelm people and reduce conversions). Amazon does this really well with their CTA: "If you like this, you might also like..." At the end of a blog, after your main call to action to get in touch, this second CTA with a list of other blogs on the topic can be extremely effective. Anyone thinking, "I'm not quite ready to make contact just yet..." will appreciate this alternative option to spend a bit more time with you first.

2. Make sure the call to action stands out.

If your call to action is hidden amongst the rest of your copy, people will miss it. Make sure it stands out so it's obvious what you want people to do next. Use a bold font or turn it into a button or image. This will grab the attention of anyone who is scan-reading the page. Remember, you're trying to make it as easy as possible for people to take the next step, so look at your page (or piece of marketing) and think to yourself, "How can I make it easier for my customers to say 'yes' to the next step I'm offering them?"

3. FILED FOR LATER

In some buyer journeys (including mine!) there's a stage where customers know that they'll need something in the future but they're not ready just yet. I call this stage "filed for later", because your customer may have noticed you, and they're interested, but they're not ready to move forward in their buyer journey for whatever reason. In my business, I notice people often think, "Yes, I'm going to need some help with our strategy... just as soon as we've landed this big contract/recruited that key team member/moved offices/other reason." They know they don't have the headspace right now, but at some point in the future they will.

The 'filed for later' stage may come before or after 'interested,' depending on your business. In my own business, customers often move back and forth between these stages for a little while before proceeding (so when I'm building my buyer journey map, 'filed for later' comes before 'interested', but this is not the case in every business) . Observe your customers' behaviour and consider when and whether this applies.

It's important to support people at this stage because, left alone, they may well forget about you. Then, when they're in a position to move forward in their decision, you won't be the person they think of.

So how do you support people at this stage?

Social media is an excellent tool for this. Encouraging people to follow you or connect with you on social media will mean they'll see your posts in their feed. They'll gradually build trust in your business over time and, when they're in a position to buy, you'll be front of mind.

Another good way of keeping in contact with potential customers is via email. Depending on your audience, you may want to email them weekly, fortnightly, monthly or even quarterly. A few businesses successfully email their list every day, but be mindful of your audience and their expectations around email etiquette. I unsubscribe from anyone who emails me daily so consider your audience and — if you're sure your audience wants frequent communications — give them the choice of a weekly or monthly digest so they don't have to choose all or nothing. It's also important to make sure you're constantly delivering value with every communication. A high-quality monthly email, with valuable content and information, is often much more effective than a daily email that's never read.

If you establish a regular rhythm of creating marketing content then repurposing your monthly or fortnightly blog into an email newsletter can be a quick and valuable task. If your email platform allows it, you can also create a welcome email, with links to your best content, to be sent automatically to new subscribers.

At every opportunity, you want to try to prompt people to realise that they need your product or service now and not at some uncertain time in the future. When planning activities for the Filed For Later stage, keep in mind the "Sparks" we identified in your Value Proposition and consider how you might be able to nudge people to realise that they need what you offer now. Remind them of the implications of delaying their decision.

For example, a blog, quiz or checklist entitled, 'Feeling stuck? Here's how to decide if [Product/Service] is right for you', or, 'Still on the fence? Here's what you need to know before deciding on [product/service]' might help someone realise that they need to stop procrastinating on this decision.

As I've said before, if any of these ideas sound like they'd make it easier for your customers to buy from you, add them to your buyer journey map and we will prioritise at the end.

4. SUPPORTING CONSIDERATION

Continuing further along your buyer journey, you now have your buyer's attention and they've started to build up some trust with you. You've delivered value and they've spent some time getting to know you.

At this point, your marketing needs to reassure customers that you're trustworthy by providing evidence of credibility and authority. Here are a few ways you can do this:

- Case studies
- Testimonials and reviews
- Awards
- Qualifications, certifications, standards, accreditations, memberships
- Statistics and facts (e.g. satisfaction ratings, uptime stats etc.)
- A guarantee
- Big-name clients
- Third-party articles about you (PR)
- Third-party endorsements

Again, this is all to support your most risk-averse buyers — signpost these pieces of evidence where your more cautious buyers can find them and be reassured.

Now your potential customer is getting serious about their purchase, weighing up the pros and cons to make sure they make the right decision.

They might have lots of questions or objections that need to be over-come for them to move forward in their decision. There might also be other people involved in the buying decision that have their own objections.

A lot of businesses leave it up to their sales team to overcome objections, but there's a lot that Marketing can do to make the job of Sales much easier. For example:

- Include common objections in your testimonials and case studies.
- A "Frequently Asked Questions" page, PDF or series of videos.
- A "Buyer's Guide".

A buyer's guide is a piece of content that educates your buyer, answers their likely questions and overcomes some or all of their objections. A good buyer's guide will be balanced and impartial. The aim is not to sell but to...

1. Empower your buyers to feel equipped to make an informed decision.
2. Filter out people who aren't right for you.
3. Deliver real value and build trust and confidence in you and your product or service.

Your buyer's guide might take the form of a well laid-out PDF, a printed booklet, a video (or series), a blog, an infographic, or any other media format. Personally, I find it's often easier to start with a written document while you play around with the structure and content, and then turn it into other formats afterwards. I know other marketers who prefer to start with a presentation. Whatever format you start with, make the most of it by recycling it into other media types so it's accessible for people with different preferences.

When choosing a topic for your buyer's guide, always refer back to your ideal customer. What would help this person feel equipped to make an informed decision?

Buyer's guides are often a great opportunity to demonstrate how you're different from other alternatives and filter out people who aren't right for you. For example, 'How to choose a graphic designer' might describe what you can expect to pay for different levels of experience. This will filter out people who don't have the budget for your services and mean you're not wasting time nurturing prospects who will never be good customers for you. It also sets your customer's expectations early on so they're not disappointed or disgruntled later on.

Buyer's guides can also give you the opportunity to equip your buyer to avoid the mistake of buying from cowboys in your industry. For example, 'The 10 things to ask your IT support company before you buy' helps buyers feel confident they can make a good buying decision for something they may not be knowledgeable about.

A buyer's guide doesn't just have to be for your buyer either. If there are several people involved in the buying decision, it's often useful to provide a buyer's guide for specific influencers or gatekeepers, e.g. 'The FD's guide to outsourcing software development', or, 'The CEO's guide to mental health awareness training'.

These pieces of content allow buyers to overcome the most common objections before they speak to anyone in Sales. This means they're much more likely to buy once they get in contact and your sales process becomes more efficient.

All of the above pieces of content can be made available in print, digital PDF, audio or video. Ideally you'd have your best content available in more than one format, again, to be accessible to people with different content preferences.

Do you have a "pizza menu"?

Sales trainer Anthony Stears once told me a story about how he bumped into his pizza menu delivery guy one day as he was leaving his house. It was a random time like Tuesday at 11am and the delivery guy was apologetic — "Sorry, I know you're not hungry for pizza right now, so just shove this in a drawer and when you *are* next hungry for pizza, have a look at what we can deliver to you."

Anthony said this is how you should approach cold-calling: "I know you're not looking for what I'm offering right now, but I have this piece of valuable content that you might find useful at some point when you want what I offer. Would you like me to send you a copy?"

This mindset will transform your sales and marketing. Instead of feeling under pressure to sell your services, you've already told them you know they're not ready to buy and so the pressure's off. And if you have the right piece of content, this conversation opener will filter out people who are unlikely to become a customer. I know if I offer someone a free guide called, 'How to attract amazing customers' and they say, "No thanks", then they'll probably never need or want what I'm selling.

So do you have a 'pizza menu' for your business? Do you have a valuable piece of content that anyone who might consider buying from you would say yes to? The best pizza menus solve a specific problem for your audience while they are considering whether or not they might want to buy from you. They may not have that problem right now, but if they can conceive that they might have that problem in the future then they'll likely accept the free content and save it for when they are 'hungry'.

For example, one of my clients is Mental Health in the Workplace (MHW). They work with large organisations to improve the wellbeing and productivity of employees and safeguard their employees' mental health. When we looked at their ideal customer persona, we realised that their prospective customers weren't making the link that the problems they were dealing with in the organisation were all caused by a systemic mental health problem among their workforce. So MHW made a quiz for HR professionals: 'Is your organisation doing enough to promote positive mental health at work?' The quiz asked people to tick which of 12 different statements they agreed with. The statements were things like, "People don't feel that their working time can be flexible and/or that they can decide when to take a break" and, "People don't feel clear on what's expected of them and/or how to get their work done."

Most were not obviously about mental health, but ticking off lots of items in the quiz prompted HR managers to have a 'spark' moment. Before doing this quiz, MHW's ideal customer may not have realised they have a mental health problem. By completing the quiz they would think, "Oh dear, we might actually have a problem here." And MHW was then perfectly placed to help with that.

The first version of MHW's quiz was a very simple PDF where you could count up your ticks and read how you fared. At the bottom, it explained if you had one to three ticks then mental wellbeing is obviously valued in your organisation — well done. If you ticked four to eight statements, then you may have some signs of work-related stress (and it gave some examples), and if you had more than nine then you likely had a serious problem. Since then, MHW have made the quiz more sophisticated using a digital platform, but the idea is the same, and it's been an incredibly effective tool for them.

Quizzes make excellent 'pizza menus' because they're engaging and people love to discover things about themselves, their lives or their businesses. Other good pizza menus include checklists, templates, cheatsheets, guides or extended how-to articles. Case studies can make good pizza menus if the angle is about how the reader could replicate the success of the subject and/or learn from their mistakes.

The key questions to ask when considering whether something would make a good pizza menu is:

1. Does it demonstrate your knowledge and help buyers to educate themselves in your area of expertise?
2. Is it genuinely valuable to your ideal customer?

The best pizza menus are the ones that help people get unstuck and give them a glimmer of confidence that the "towards" you're offering is achievable for them. Some example titles to start with include:

- "The ultimate guide to..."
- "X questions to ask before you hire a..."
- "How to choose a..."
- "X unexpected signs you might need a..."
- "How to build a business case for XYZ"
- "X mistakes people make when..."
- "Do I need X or Y?"
- "The [job role]'s guide to..."

- "X things to do/have in place before starting your next project"

How to recycle your content

Recycling your pizza menu into other forms of content is another way you can actively support your ideal customers while they are still considering their buying decision. These longer pieces of content can be a bit of an investment to create in a small business, so you want to make sure you get the biggest bang for your buck.

Here are some ideas for different ways you can recycle this long-form content:

- Chop it up and rewrite it into a number of smaller blogs: one about each subheading, that all encourage people to request the larger piece of content.
- Create social media posts or reels about each blog and remember to pin your best content to your page or profile.
- Create short (one to three minutes depending on your topic and audience) videos about different aspects of the topic.
- Create a presentation on the topic and record yourself presenting it, or create a video tutorial on it.
- Create an infographic or animated video about the topic.
- Create a podcast series on the topic.
- Send it to leads who are currently interested in buying, or to leads who have gone cold to 'rewarm' them.
- Create a 'link tree' (a mobile-friendly page with a list of links) directing users to your key pieces of content.
- When someone books a call with you, send them the pizza menu or one of these variants to give them something to ponder in the meantime. Give it some context in order to help them prepare for this call with you and to understand what to expect.

- Use your pizza menu as an excuse to reach out to past customers to invite them back into your orbit: "We've just published this new piece of content and I thought you might find it useful. Let me know what you think. Here's a link to my diary if you have a moment to chat."

5. ENCOURAGING THE FIRST PURCHASE

For many customers, the first moment they hand over their money can feel a bit risky. Hopefully, by the time they get to this stage, you've built trust through your content and sales process. But is there anything more you can do to make that first purchase feel easier? How can you reduce the perceived risk at this stage? The key is to help your customers understand exactly what it will be like to be a customer *before* they make the purchase.

Explain what will happen when they buy

To reduce perceived risk, it's essential that your customers know what will happen when they buy from you. This is often overlooked, especially by service-based businesses that have been working in their industry for years. If you're an expert in your field, it's easy to forget that your customers may not know what to expect. Take a moment to think through the process you take new customers through. How does the actual sale occur? What information will you ask them to provide? What happens once they've made their payment? How is their purchase delivered, and what happens next?

Answer the all-important question: *How and when will I get value from this?* For many product sales, this might be as simple as telling customers how long it will take to assemble a product and what tools are needed. But for services, where it can take longer for customers to see value, creating content that explains the process between handing over money and receiving value is a great way to alleviate concerns. For some businesses, the process may vary considerably from one customer to another but there are usually common milestones.

145

One of the best ways to do this is by creating a clear, visual flow of your process. This could be a blog post, a guide, an infographic, or a video that outlines the journey your customer will go through. I worked with a graphic designer who created a beautiful flow diagram for his process: starting with a discovery call, moving through concept development, and ending with the final delivery. Displaying this on his website helped prospective clients understand exactly what would happen once they reached out, and when the process went exactly as described, it built even more trust and confidence.

This is especially important for services where the value isn't immediate. If you can show your customers what the process will look like, you help them feel more confident about their decision.

Let your customers have a "test drive"

Your customers also need to understand what it will *feel* like to be a customer before they commit. Just like you wouldn't buy a car without test-driving it first, your customers need a chance to try you out before handing over their money.

For product businesses, this could be as simple as offering a product demo or a video tour. For SaaS or membership businesses, it could be a free trial. Even for service businesses, the test drive is still possible. Every meeting, proposal, or presentation is an opportunity for the customer to experience how you treat your clients. If you send out proposals, consider including a relevant case study or testimonial that explains how a past client felt about their experience with you. This not only shows how your service works but also gives a sense of how they might feel as your customer.

Reducing the perceived risk of high-value purchases

When you're selling high-ticket items, customers may feel more risk-averse. This is where a product ladder can come in handy. A product ladder is a series of smaller offers or products that gradually lead to the larger purchase. The idea is to build trust and help your customer get comfortable with you before they commit to something big. Here's an example of what this could look like:

1. Free short-form content (blog posts, videos etc) with a call to action that leads to...
2. A free offer (such as a PDF or trial in exchange for an email address) that invites people to book or watch...
3. A product or service demonstration (either in person, remotely or via video) to give buyers a chance to test drive your offering before...
4. A "taster" product (a low-cost, fixed-price, entry-level product or package of services) that leads on to...
5. Your core product or service offering.

If your service is tailored, it's tough to give an exact price upfront. But a fixed-price "taster" package, like a discovery or scoping package, lets customers experience your service while also providing them with a clear idea of your price point. A taster package not only reduces the perceived risk and eases them gently into becoming a customer, but also helps customers gauge where you fall on the pricing spectrum. Are you a budget offering, a premium option, or somewhere in between? This transparency is essential. No one wants to be blindsided by a price that's far higher than expected. When the price feels out of line with what they anticipated, customers not only feel uncomfortable and frustrated, but it can also activate their Chimp brain, which might sabotage the sale.

By offering a taster package, customers get a clear idea of what they're getting, both in terms of service and cost, which helps set realistic expectations for the full, tailored package. They'll have a much clearer sense of whether or not they can afford you, which reduces discomfort and increases the likelihood of them moving forward.

If you're really unable to create a fixed-price taster offering, consider costing up scenarios and publishing these prices as examples. It'll help your customers know what to expect if they have, say, three example scenarios priced up. They can look at these prices and think, "What I want is in between scenario one and scenario two so it'll probably cost around..." This reassurance reduces their perceived risk of moving forwards in their decision and getting in contact with you.

Setting the right price is one of the most important decisions small businesses make. It directly impacts your profitability, customer perception, and overall success. Pricing has an important effect on your buyer journey, but in the interest of keeping this section streamlined, I've included an Appendix at the back of the book that takes a deep dive into pricing strategies. Pricing isn't a one-size-fits-all approach, so I highly recommend taking some time to read through it once you've finished this chapter. The pricing strategy you choose should reflect your market, your product or service's value, and your long-term goals, and can have a profound impact on how your ideal customers perceive your business.

6. CULTIVATING LOYALTY

This is a really important moment in your customer's buying journey — immediately after they've handed over cash or signed on the dotted line. If you've ever experienced buyer's remorse, you'll know what happens if a buyer's emotional needs aren't met at this point.

Your marketing needs to reassure your buyer they've made the right choice. Greet customers with a lovely warm welcome to build an emotional connection and prevent buyer's remorse. This doesn't have to be complicated and what you decide is appropriate will depend on your business, industry and sale value.

A low-value, transactional sale needs little more than a personalised email confirmation. Having said that, I've received products ordered from small businesses online that had clearly been carefully wrapped by hand and a little hand-written card added to the package, and this was much appreciated.

For relational sales, a simple hand-written welcome card or gift shows customers that you care about them. In some industries, a gift may not be appropriate, but a thank-you card really stands out. I've also seen businesses send personalised video messages to welcome new clients, which is really effective and takes only a couple of minutes if you have a script template you use with each one. If you're thinking, "No one in our industry does anything like this — it'd be weird if we did," consider how you'd feel as a customer if a supplier took the time to thank you.

Chances are, you'd appreciate it. Sometimes standing out is exactly what makes the difference.

As well as your customer's emotional needs, they also have logical needs at this stage. If you're selling something even slightly complex, your customer may not be 100% sure what they've bought into. Now is the time to remind them exactly what they've paid for and what they're going to get. Earlier in this chapter I talked about creating a piece of content that explains how you work and the process your customer will go through now that they've made their purchase. Now is the time to send this to them (again, if they've already received it) so they can see where they are in the process and what's going to happen next.

Remember, it may be obvious to you because you know your business so well, but your customer may not have been through a process like this before, so they may get lost. Think of this piece of content like the signage you see when you're halfway through a forest trail with a big "YOU ARE HERE" arrow on it. Even if you have a paper copy of a map in your hand (or Google Maps on your phone) it's still reassuring to know you're not lost.

A lot of businesses consider all this post-sale support to be the sole responsibility of Customer Services, Account Management, or possibly Operations, and so Marketing misses the opportunity to have an impact here. But if we go back to my original definition of marketing as "making it really easy for people to buy" then anything that makes it easier for people to buy *more* is also marketing. Whether these activities are carried out by your marketing team or your after-sales team doesn't matter. What's important is ensuring the customer's buyer journey is seamless, easy and comfortable.

Onboarding is a crucial part of the buyer journey, especially if your product or service requires any learning curve, like software or technical tools. A smooth onboarding process ensures customers know how to get the most value from what they've bought. This might include training sessions, user guides, or even just a friendly check-in call to answer any questions. And let's not forget the importance of quickly resolving any hiccups. Issues left unresolved can undo all the goodwill you've worked so hard to build. Think of onboarding as your chance to turn a buyer into a confident user who's already looking forward to buying from you again.

You'd be amazed at the number of businesses I've worked with who forget to look after and support their loyal customers. Loyal customers are your most profitable buyers — you've already spent the money to acquire them, so subsequent purchases are much more profitable because you don't have that up-front cost anymore. Make sure you maintain the relationship you've built through their buyer journey and keep the magic alive.

Nurturing customers over the long term is all about consistency and care. Your brand visuals and tone of voice should feel like a familiar friend — reassuring and recognisable in every interaction, from a customer-only newsletter packed with tips and updates, to the way you respond to support queries. There's a lot of psychology behind this: subtle inconsistencies erode trust and cause your once-loyal customer to lose their emotional connection with your brand.

Regular communication (as is appropriate without annoying them) keeps customers in the loop about service changes, new features, or special offers just for them. But nurturing isn't just about broadcasting — it's about listening, too. Proactively seeking feedback shows you care about improving their experience and builds trust. Small gestures, like a Christmas card (or gift for higher value customers) or a thoughtful thank-you gift, can make customers feel truly valued. And of course, nurturing is the perfect opportunity to introduce customers to other products or services that could benefit them, through well-timed upselling (selling more of the same product or service) or cross-selling (selling other products or services you offer). Just make sure that it feels helpful, not pushy. The goal is simple: to show your customers they're not just a transaction — they're part of your business's journey.

Nurturing long-term customer relationships isn't just about main-taining consistency; it's also about staying in touch and keeping the conversation alive. Content is a powerful way to do this. Whether it's a new blog, video, or podcast, any new content is a perfect excuse to re-engage with customers who may have slipped through the cracks. A simple message like, "Hi [Customer Name], it's been a while, I hope you're well. I've just posted this new blog/video/podcast and thought of you. Let me know if it's useful!" can remind them that you're still here, offering value.

Content also gives you more opportunities to upsell or cross-sell. If you're sharing information about a new product or service, remember to mention how it might benefit existing customers. A quick email saying, "Did you know we also offer X? Here's a bit of info about it in case it could be useful for you..." is an easy way to introduce customers to more of what you have to offer without being pushy.

If you really want to go above and beyond to nurture loyalty in your customer base, think about how you can create personalised experiences that make your customers feel truly valued. Personalisation can be as simple as remembering their preferences, offering tailored recommendations, or acknowledging milestones like birthdays or anniversaries. When customers feel like you understand them and their needs, they're more likely to stick around. A personalised email or a special offer on a customer's anniversary with your brand can go a long way in strengthening that bond. We love choosing a personal gift for our valued clients at Christmas to show them how important they have been to us over the past year.

Another way to deepen loyalty is by fostering a sense of community. Loyalty is often driven by connection, not just to your product but to other customers who share similar experiences. Consider creating exclusive spaces, like private groups or forums, where customers can engage with each other and share tips, feedback, or stories. Hosting online events or webinars just for loyal customers also helps build a community where customers feel like they're part of something bigger than a transaction.

Exclusive access or VIP treatment is another powerful loyalty booster. Whether it's early access to new products or services, priority customer support, or customer-only content and events, giving your loyal customers something extra shows them they're more than just another sale. People love feeling like they're part of an exclusive group, and it keeps them invested in your brand.

Finally, don't just wait for customers to come to you with problems — be proactive in your approach. Regular check-ins or follow-ups to see how customers are enjoying your product or service not only shows that you care, but it helps you catch any issues before they escalate. If customers know they can rely on you for support, they'll feel more confident sticking with your brand long-term.

7. INCENTIVISING REFERRALS

Isn't it wonderful when your happy, loyal customers are generating new business for you? Referrals are one of the most powerful tools for acquiring new customers, because that referral builds a level of trust with the prospective customer. Yet so many businesses miss the opportunity to encourage their customers to refer them. Many think that referrals happen naturally and are outside their control, but the truth is, with a little effort, you can encourage more referrals to come your way. The first step is simply to ask!

If your customers are already loyal to you then they'll probably be happy to tell other people about you. But people are busy and sometimes they need a gentle nudge to do this. Having a process for reaching out to existing customers and asking if they know anyone who might benefit from your product or service is a great way to start. You can frame it like this: *"We really love working with you. By any chance, do you know anyone in a similar situation to you who might also benefit from what we offer?"* A gentle prompt can often lead to new opportunities.

Tracking referrals and thanking those who send them your way is equally important. Let your referrers know they are valued, whether it's through a simple thank-you email or something more tangible, like a small gift. It's essential that referrers feel appreciated for their efforts, as this not only strengthens your relationship with them but encourages them to keep referring to you.

You can also offer incentives for successful referrals. A thank-you can go a long way and there are lots of examples to inspire you. Think about Ocado's "£10 for you and £10 for a friend" and Dropbox's "earn more space by inviting a friend". I particularly like strategies like this, where both the referrer and the referee get a benefit, because it helps ensure both parties feel good about your business and neither party feels exploited. This balance makes the process feel rewarding and fair.

A highly effective referral tactic is to make it as easy as possible for your customers to recommend you. One way to do this is by providing a ready-to-use email template they can send to potential leads. Instead of asking them to directly refer you (which might feel awkward if they're unsure whether the recipient needs your services) you can offer a template like this:

> "Hi [Name], I know a marketing professional who works with businesses like yours. She has some free resources I've found really helpful, and I thought you might find them useful too. Here's the link... [insert links to valuable content]."

This approach takes the pressure off the referrer and simplifies the process, making it much easier for them to spread the word.

New content is also a fantastic way to re-engage referrers. When you post something useful, reach out to your referrers and ask if they know anyone who might benefit from it. For instance, you could say,

> "Hi [Name], I know you work with clients in [industry]. I've just posted this blog [link], and I thought it might be helpful for some of your clients. Would you mind passing it along if you think of anyone who would find it useful?"

This way, you're giving them something of value to share while prompting a referral.

Lastly, if you attend networking events or presentations, make sure to mention key pieces of content and encourage your audience to think of someone who might find it helpful. Whether it's a video tutorial, guide, or blog post, when you tie your content to a potential referral, it gives people a reason to share it.

Don't overlook the power of content as a tool for referrals. Whenever you create something valuable, take the opportunity to ask your loyal customers if they know anyone who might benefit from it. It's a subtle but effective way to generate referrals without feeling like you're directly asking for them.

———

END OF CHAPTER CHECKLIST

I have:

☐ Added all my ideas for improving my buyer journey to my buyer journey map.

☐ Identified the areas of the buyer journey where I have the most opportunity for improvement.

☐ Identified key pieces of content to create that will support buyers along their journey.

CHAPTER 10
PRIORITISE, PLAN, PROPEL

When it comes to marketing, it's easy to get overwhelmed. The possibilities are endless, with new ideas, platforms, and strategies popping up constantly. One of my clients referred to this as the "marketing smorgasbord". At first, this can feel exciting — there are so many ways to reach your audience and grow your business! But when it's time to take action, that abundance of options can quickly become overwhelming. When faced with an endless list of potential tactics, the pressure to do it all can be paralysing. Without clear priorities, the noise of all those ideas can drown out what really matters, making it hard to focus on what will actually move the needle for your business.

This is why setting marketing priorities is essential. It's not about doing everything — it's about doing what will have the biggest impact. So before you even consider starting any of the marketing activities we've talked about in the earlier chapter, make sure you prioritise first. Even a simple one-page plan, with your top 10 tasks in priority order, will enable you to overcome your overwhelm by focusing only on your #1 task. Don't even look at task #2 until you've done #1 — just work through the list one task at a time.

So how do you prioritise? In practice there are many methods for prioritisation, some more complicated than others, and I'll go through my favourite method in this chapter. The important thing is that, whatever method you choose, it must be logical and trustworthy. Without a logical method for prioritisation, we're left to rely on "gut feel" to effectively guess which marketing activity should be our top priority. And let me tell you, my gut is about as reliable as a weather forecast — it might say one thing one day and something entirely different the next. When we leave our marketing decisions up to chance like this, we end up hopping from one idea to the next without giving any of them the attention they deserve. Or, we focus on things that we like or feel comfortable with, while putting off the tasks we're not confident executing.

If you spend ages deciding, or you keep switching from one thing to another to another and not completing anything, it will kill your progress. What we really need is a method we can trust to guide us through our decision-making, so we can tackle the most impactful activities first and follow through on them.

Having a prioritised marketing plan is like batch cooking your meals for the week. On a Sunday afternoon, it might take me a couple of hours to prepare all my meals. But if I cooked everything from scratch every evening, I'd end up spending at least twice that amount of time in total. The upfront investment in time pays off because it makes the rest of the week so much more efficient. It's the same with marketing. Taking the time to set a strategy and create a plan makes your marketing activities far more effective. Without it, we risk letting urgent tasks take over, leaving crucial activities on the back burner.

Another benefit of batch cooking is that it helps me ensure my family gets a balanced diet, instead of ending up eating cheesy pasta for dinner every night. With a solid marketing plan, I can ensure a balanced approach to my activities, making sure I don't overlook important elements in the rush of day-to-day tasks. Once you have a prioritised plan in place, the vast majority of your marketing becomes easy, because you don't have to think through every little decision. Those decisions have already been made and are based on logical, robust rationale.

And when you get a curve-ball, like when someone calls you up with a "great marketing opportunity" out of the blue, you'll be able to quickly decide if it fits in with the rest of your marketing and will deliver a return on your investment, or if it'll actually be a complete waste of time and money.

One of my favourite client prioritisation success stories comes from a design agency called Amperative. Back in early March 2020, I was working with them to create a 90-day marketing plan. We had just developed an excellent strategy, and everyone on the team had a clear understanding of how they were going to meet their goals over the next three months.

Then two weeks later, the world changed dramatically. The UK went into lockdown because of Covid-19. With a call already scheduled for the following week, I anticipated I might be speaking to a stressed and overwhelmed team. After all, so many businesses were grappling with the sudden and unpredictable shifts in their markets. But when I spoke to Amperative, I was pleasantly surprised. Instead of panic, I found calm.

Amperative was able to pivot quickly because they already had a well-considered marketing plan and a clear picture of their ideal client. They might have had an initial moment of panic, but then they took a step back, assessed the shifting landscape, and adjusted their content strategy to address their ideal customer's concerns in the moment. The steps they'd laid out in their plan remained unchanged — only the focus of their content shifted to be more relevant to the uncertainty and challenges their audience was facing.

By investing time upfront in a solid strategy, Amperative didn't have to throw everything out the window when things changed. They didn't panic or blindly copy their competitors' responses to the crisis. Instead, they used their deep understanding of their ideal customer to create content that resonated. Within about an hour, they identified their customers' biggest challenges and concerns related to the lockdown, and they created content that spoke directly to those issues.

For example, they published blogs like, 'The 4 Stages of Transition as a Business Owner and Parent in Lockdown' and 'Making a Pitch to a Creative Agency During Lockdown'. This proactive approach to adjusting their content ensured they stayed connected with their audience, rather than churning out irrelevant posts. By sticking to their strategy and adjusting tactically, Amperative were able to ride out the uncertainty and maintain a strong connection with their customers.

This is why having a 90-day action plan is crucial to moving your marketing strategy forward. It allows you to take all the ideas you've had for improving your buyer journey and implement them in a predictable, achievable way, reducing overwhelm by keeping the focus on the near-term, and allowing you to be dynamic in responding to what's happening for your ideal customers.

For the rest of this chapter, we'll be looking at how to build both 90-day action plans and rolling 90-day plans. Both are essential tools for effective marketing, but they serve different purposes. Action plans are perfect for tackling one-off projects that need focused attention and a clear deadline, while rolling plans keep your regular marketing activities on track and ensure consistency over time. By combining these two approaches, you can strike the right balance between making progress on big goals and maintaining the day-to-day tasks that drive long-term success.

HOW TO PRIORITISE INTO A ONE-PAGE PLAN

The first step of building your 90-day action plan is to create a one-page plan to start working from. To do this, you'll need to have your buyer journey map in front of you, so you can see where all the gaps in your marketing are and the new ideas you've added. These new ideas are the "marketing smorgasbord" we're going to prioritise now.

I've used a lot of different prioritisation methods over the years but now I mainly use two methods in combination, which I'll describe in this chapter.

There are a few exceptions which I'll cover later, but this combination covers most situations, and there are two steps:

1. Quick wins
2. Conversion first

Using these two methods (in that order!) will give you a prioritised, one-page action plan that you can start implementing straight away.

QUICK WINS

I always start with this and you'll see why: it's quick and creates a short list of things you can complete in a few hours that will start making an impact on your sales.

The reason I start with quick wins is that they're motivating. When you start ticking them off and seeing how easy it can be to make meaningful improvements to your marketing, you'll want to do more of it. Ticking off a number of tasks also gives you a boost of dopamine (one of our "happy hormones") that will keep you motivated when you start to tackle the harder topics.

So, for each of the marketing tasks you've identified, ask yourself:

1. Can this be implemented in less than an hour?
2. Will this make it easier for customers to buy?

If the answer to both is yes, add it to your quick wins list.

The order in which you work through this list is not really important, because these tasks don't take long to implement. The important thing is to get them done quickly. If you find you have a lot of quick wins (hooray!) you could put your shortlist through the "conversion first" method below to prioritise them for maximum profitability, but most of the time that's not necessary.

Don't waste time on this: they're quick wins so get them done as soon as you can. Re-prioritising a to-do list is a procrastination tactic I can spot a mile away... mainly because it's one of my own shortcomings!

CONVERSION FIRST

This method was inspired by Bryony Thomas's 'Watertight Marketing' prioritisation method. She created a beautifully simple method, prioritising activities from the end of the buyer journey (or the "bottom of the funnel", in her description) forwards towards the start. I've adapted her method to fit my own purposes.

This method is based on the principle that lead-generation activities are generally more expensive than conversion-improving activities.

The cost of driving more traffic to your website is roughly proportional to the number of people you want to reach. This is absolutely true if you're doing any "pay per lead" activity such as digital advertising (pay per click) or direct mailing (pay per stamp!). Even in other lead generation activities like print advertising, PR, exhibitions or networking, it's generally true that the more time and money you spend, the more leads you should get. Marketing budgets make a big difference here.

Later on down the buyer journey, however, your marketing tasks are aiming at increasing conversion. Whether you have 50 people or 50,000 people reading a piece of content, it doesn't much change the cost of producing that piece of content.

It makes sense, therefore, to work on your conversion-improving activities first, before you increase your spend on lead generation. If you're spending lots of money on lead generation but those people aren't converting into customers then you're wasting that money.

It's also important to remember that your marketing is all about laying a path for your customers to walk. If you build your path from the customer and work towards your business, your customers will start walking the path, but if the path isn't finished then all those potential customers will reach a point where their buying journey becomes difficult or frustrating. They'll have a bad buying experience and may well decide never to buy from you again. Worse, they may tell others about their poor experience.

This is why you build your path to purchase starting at the end and working backwards, towards the customer. It doesn't have to be perfect, but it has to be functional.

Here's how to do it.

1. If you haven't already, map out your buyer journey by making a list of your buyer journey stages and, for each stage, list your current marketing and add any new marketing ideas.
2. For each idea, look at how much you need to support your customers at that stage and consider, from your customer's perspective, the decision to move to the next stage. How much risk is there? If the risk is relatively high and you don't have much to support your customers at this stage then you need to put something in place. If you have a few ideas to choose from, consider what will build the most trust for your customer. Put a star next to the ideas that you think will make the biggest impact or, if you're doing this digitally, make your post-it note red.
3. For the new ideas that won't make as much of an impact, put a smaller mark on the post-it or, if digital, make your post-it amber.
4. When you've done this for every stage, start at the end of your buyer journey and work your way backwards. Find the first starred (or red) marketing task (the one closest to the end of the buyer journey). This is your top marketing task. Write this on your one-page marketing plan under your 'quick wins' section. Continue through your list (working your way towards the beginning of your buyer journey) adding all your red, or starred, tasks to your marketing plan.
5. Once you've prioritised all your top-priority tasks, go back to the end of your buyer journey and revisit your list looking at your amber tasks. Add these in order on to your marketing

plan, again, starting at the end of the buyer journey and working backwards to the beginning.

A WORKED EXAMPLE

Here's an example buyer journey I mapped out using the process I described earlier (and if you need to read the notes on the post-its, please revisit the double-page image on pages 74–75):

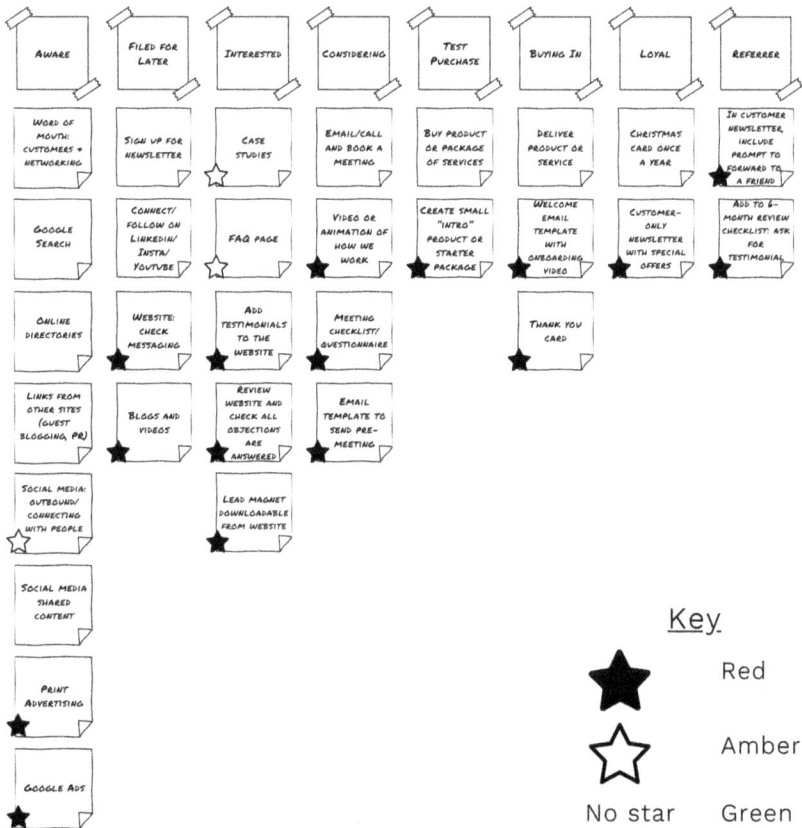

AWARE	FILED FOR LATER	INTERESTED	CONSIDERING	TEST PURCHASE	BUYING IN	LOYAL	REFERRER
WORD OF MOUTH: CUSTOMERS + NETWORKING	SIGN UP FOR NEWSLETTER	CASE STUDIES ☆	EMAIL/CALL AND BOOK A MEETING	BUY PRODUCT OR PACKAGE OF SERVICES	DELIVER PRODUCT OR SERVICE	CHRISTMAS CARD ONCE A YEAR	IN CUSTOMER NEWSLETTER, INCLUDE PROMPT TO FORWARD TO A FRIEND ★
GOOGLE SEARCH	CONNECT/ FOLLOW ON LINKEDIN/ INSTA/ YOUTUBE	FAQ PAGE ☆	VIDEO OR ANIMATION OF HOW WE WORK	CREATE SMALL "INTRO" PRODUCT OR STARTER PACKAGE ★	WELCOME EMAIL TEMPLATE WITH ONBOARDING VIDEO ★	CUSTOMER-ONLY NEWSLETTER WITH SPECIAL OFFERS ★	ADD TO 6-MONTH REVIEW CHECKLIST: ASK FOR TESTIMONIAL
ONLINE DIRECTORIES	WEBSITE: CHECK MESSAGING ★	ADD TESTIMONIALS TO THE WEBSITE ★	MEETING CHECKLIST/ QUESTIONNAIRE		THANK YOU CARD ★		
LINKS FROM OTHER SITES (GUEST BLOGGING, PR)	BLOGS AND VIDEOS	REVIEW WEBSITE AND CHECK ALL OBJECTIONS ARE ANSWERED ★	EMAIL TEMPLATE TO SEND PRE-MEETING ★				
SOCIAL MEDIA: OUTBOUND/ CONNECTING WITH PEOPLE ☆		LEAD MAGNET DOWNLOADABLE FROM WEBSITE ★					
SOCIAL MEDIA SHARED CONTENT							
PRINT ADVERTISING ★							
GOOGLE ADS ★							

Key

★ Red

☆ Amber

No star   Green

The green post-its (with no star), along with our resources and processes, are already in place. As you can see, we're already ranking fairly well on Google, we're on the most important online directories, our social media content is being shared and reaching new people, etc.

I've added red post-its (with a black star in the image above) for all my new ideas. We know these things will make it easier for people to buy from us and we currently have nothing in place.

Lastly, I've also added a few amber post-its (with a white star on the image above). These are either lower-impact activities or things we have in place but we know they could be better. We have an FAQs page but, having done a thorough customer persona, we've realised there are quite a few questions we want to add. The most important ones are there but it needs some tweaks. Our case studies are a bit out of date and we stopped connecting with people on LinkedIn because we were busy and weren't convinced it was delivering ROI. However, with our metrics in place, we're now more confident we could make it profitable.

First, we pick out the quick wins: the tasks that can be done in one hour or less.

Ignoring any other priorities for the moment, our quick wins are:

1. Check messaging on the website and make obvious tweaks to headlines.
2. Add additional FAQs to the FAQs page.
3. Review website against our list of objections and check all are covered (if quick, add any outstanding objections to the FAQs page).
4. Create a checklist of questions for our initial meeting with a prospective customer.
5. Create an email template with prep for the meeting, to send to prospects when they book an initial call.
6. Create an email template welcoming new customers.
7. Create a script for a personalised onboarding video (to record using something like Zoom or Loom) that welcomes new customers and gives them the information they need to get started.
8. Buy a pack of unbranded thank-you cards.
9. Set up an automated reminder process and checklist for a six-month review, that prompts us to ask for a testimonial.

Since each one of those tasks will take less than an hour, we can now schedule them into our diary (or delegate them to other people to get done) over the next couple of weeks. And someone's just booked an initial meeting with me, so I'm going to do the pre-meeting email template and initial meeting checklist first!

Now I've got the first nine tasks on my marketing action plan, I can prioritise the rest using "conversion first":

10. Create a customer-only newsletter with special offers for customers; include a line to the bottom to prompt readers to forward it to a friend.
11. Create a small intro or starter package to offer before the main package of services.
12. Create a video animation of how we work. If that's too big a task, or too costly, I could start with a written description or a visual graphic in a PDF, and then turn it into an animation later.
13. Create an email template to send to customers before our first meeting.
14. Review the website and ensure all objections are addressed.
15. Gather testimonials and add them to the website.
16. Create a lead magnet and add it to the website for people to download.
17. Establish a rhythm of blog and video content creation.
18. Invest in print and Google advertising to generate more awareness.
19. Update our old case studies and create new ones.
20. Establish a rhythm of proactively connecting with people on LinkedIn (or outsource this activity to an agency).

You might have noticed that tasks 14 to 16 are all in the "Interested" stage of our buyer journey, so how did I decide what order to prioritise them? I simply put them in the order of how long I think each one will take, starting with the quickest. When I get to the stage of putting these tasks into a detailed 90-day plan I'll aim to work on some of them concurrently. For example, I can be gathering testimonials from customers while working on the lead magnet.

There is an exception to this rule, and that is if you anticipate rebranding your business in the foreseeable future. If you want to avoid rework and keep your marketing costs as low as possible, then it's usually best to do your rebrand before you start creating content and updating your website and marketing materials. I know it can be frustrating putting a plan on hold while a rebrand is underway, so try to look for a few marketing improvements that won't be affected by the rebrand and implement those. Good examples for this include process improvements or gathering testimonials and case studies.

CHUNKING: HOW TO STRUCTURE A MARKETING PLAN THAT WORKS FOR YOU

Creating a marketing plan that works for your business is a balancing act. You want to include all the right information without overwhelming yourself with unnecessary details. How you should structure your plan depends on how you process and organise information, and understanding your preferences can make all the difference.

Some of us are big-picture thinkers, while others prefer to dig into the details. This concept is explained well in *Time Mastery* by Karen Meager and John McLachlan, where they discuss how we "chunk" information. Some people think in small, digestible chunks — like 30-minute time blocks — while others think in bigger units, such as days, weeks, or even years. These preferences aren't just limited to how we approach time, but also how we think about tasks and projects. Big chunkers are drawn to lofty goals, big ideas, and strategic thinking but often feel overwhelmed by details. Small chunkers, on the other hand, are happiest when working through lists of small tasks, breaking everything down into manageable steps. This is a spectrum, so you may be somewhere in the middle.

Understanding your chunking preference can help you create a marketing plan that feels natural and effective for you. Take a moment to reflect on how you typically approach tasks — do you prefer to think in big, overarching goals, or do you like breaking things into smaller, detailed steps? Do you prefer to have a weekly or monthly overview calendar or a detailed daily schedule? Do you feel most in flow when working on one big project or when ticking off a list of little tasks?

Big Chunk Marketing Plans

If you're a big-chunk thinker, you'll likely be drawn to high-level plans and strategies. Your ideal marketing plan will be shorter and more focused on the broader picture. For example, I had a client who was a classic big-chunk person, and his entire marketing plan for the year fit on less than two pages. He didn't want to be bogged down by detail; he wanted an outline that could guide him toward his goals.

The challenge with big-chunk plans, however, is execution. While a high-level plan is great for vision and direction, you also need someone who can drill down into the details to make those ideas happen. If you're a big-chunk thinker and struggle to break down projects into tasks, find a small-chunk person on your team who can help you work out the steps needed to execute your strategy.

I'm a big chunker: my marketing plan has just a few tasks per week for me to implement. I don't need to break them down into very detailed steps, as I'm happiest when I'm working on one thing for a couple of hours. "Write copy for lead magnet" is a sufficiently detailed task for me.

When you're planning your time, you may find you're most productive if you set aside a few hours once a week to work on your marketing in one big chunk.

Small Chunk Marketing Plans

On the flip side, if you're a small-chunk thinker, you'll prefer a detailed marketing plan. You'll want every task to be broken down into manageable steps. If a three-month plan feels overwhelming, mark out only your main milestones for the quarter and then do a detailed one-month plan. Each month, spend a few minutes checking your milestones and the progress you're making, and make a new detailed one-month plan.

Bear in mind that small chunkers can sometimes struggle with the strategic aspect of planning. High-level goals might feel abstract or difficult to tackle. If you've found any of the strategic aspects of this book challenging, seek help from a big chunker to help you define your overarching goals. Once you've got that big picture in place, you can happily dive back into the details of execution, breaking down your strategy into smaller, achievable actions.

Sequencer or Themer?

Another important consideration when structuring your marketing plan is how you naturally organise tasks and information. Some people instinctively think in terms of a sequence with one step logically following the next. Others prefer to group tasks into themes or categories, tackling related activities together. Neither approach is better than the other; they're just different personal preferences for processing information. Recognising which method feels more natural to you can help you create a plan that's easy to follow and stick to.

Consider whether you prefer working in a linear, step-by-step sequence, or if you're more comfortable grouping tasks into particular focus areas. If you're not sure, imagine you're describing to a friend what you've done this week. Do you start at the beginning of the week and describe Monday first, then Tuesday, then Wednesday etc? Or do you naturally think through your week in terms of categories of activities? A themer might first describe all the things they'd done with family before moving on to describe sports or leisure activities they've engaged in, what they've done in work, and then times when they've seen friends and so on.

By recognising your preferences, you can tailor your marketing plan to suit your natural way of thinking.

Sequenced Marketing Plans

A sequencer will likely prefer to organise their marketing plan structuring tasks in the order in which they'll execute them. Sequencers like to follow a clear timeline, starting with the first task and progressing step by step.

If you're a small-chunk sequencer, you might want a detailed timeline, specifying what you'll do each day in the order you'll do it. A big-chunk sequencer, however, might only focus on one major task per week or month.

Themed Marketing Plans

Themers organise their marketing efforts by categories or themes — such as content, social media, advertising, and PR. While some themers thrive in this framework, they might face challenges when it comes to prioritisation. It can be easy to get stuck in a theme and start working on a task that isn't the most important.

Once you've identified the tasks in each theme, make sure to prioritise them. If necessary, seek help from a sequencer on your team to help order tasks in terms of urgency and importance.

Remember: everyone has a degree of flexibility in this. You might find that there are some situations where you behave in a much more sequenced way when normally you are a themer, or vice versa. There may be situations where you think big-chunk when normally you prefer small-chunk, or vice versa. Everyone can flex to a degree — the important thing is to know your preference so you can play to your strengths and manage your energy levels. If we're working in a way that is not our preference, we can find ourselves feeling drained of energy much more quickly and we're less likely to enjoy the task. I want you to enjoy your marketing so, wherever possible, work in a way that suits your preferences.

Here are some examples of big chunk and small chunk marketing plans. Which one do you feel most comfortable with?

Big Chunk Marketing Plan

	Goal 1: Create a lead magnet	Goal 2: Post on LinkedIn 2 x per week
Week 1	Plan lead magnet contents	2 x LinkedIn posts
Week 2	Write lead magnet	2 x LinkedIn posts
Week 3	Write lead magnet	2 x LinkedIn posts
Week 4	Build lead magnet in Canva	2 x LinkedIn posts
Week 5	Review & edit	2 x LinkedIn posts
Week 6	Launch!	2 x LinkedIn posts

Small Chunk Marketing Plan

	Goal 1: Create a lead magnet	Goal 2: Post on LinkedIn 2 x per week
Week 1	• Create a plan • Outline the lead magnet	• Write 2 x LinkedIn posts • Share on LinkedIn (Wednesday & Friday)
Week 2	• Write sections 1 & 2 of the lead magnet • Lay out in Canva • Create supporting images	• Write 2 x LinkedIn posts • Share on LinkedIn (Tuesday & Thursday)
Week 3	• Write sections 1 & 2 of the lead magnet • Lay out in Canva • Create supporting images	• Write 2 x LinkedIn posts • Share on LinkedIn (Monday & Wednesday)
Week 4	• Write sections 1 & 2 of the lead magnet • Lay out in Canva • Create supporting images	• Write 2 x LinkedIn posts • Share on LinkedIn (Tuesday & Friday)
Week 5	• Review lead magnet • Make edits	• Write 2 x LinkedIn posts • Share on LinkedIn (Monday & Thursday)
Week 6	• Launch! • Add to the website • Write post about lead magnet and share on LinkedIn	• Write 2 x LinkedIn posts • Share on LinkedIn (Wednesday & Friday)

A ROLLING 90-DAY PLAN

Earlier in this chapter you turned your one-page plan into a 90-day action plan, and now we also need to consider your 'rolling' plan.

A rolling 90-day plan is designed for the regular, recurring activities that keep your marketing consistent and effective. These include things like writing blogs, posting on social media, producing case studies, measuring your results, and updating your website. The beauty of a rolling plan is that it doesn't need to be reinvented every quarter — it's a framework you can tweak as needed but is largely "rinse and repeat". This ensures you stay on top of ongoing marketing tasks without losing momentum or wasting time starting from scratch. By combining both types of plans strategically, you can tackle big projects while maintaining consistency in your day-to-day marketing efforts.

Here's an example of a rolling 90-day plan:

PRIORITISE, PLAN, PROPEL

	Fortnightly blog and monthly newsletter	Publish one case study per month	Keep website up to date	Social media
Week 1	Review content and plan quarter's blogs	Choose 3 subjects for case studies	Plan new evergreen marketing content to add to the website	Plan social media content
Week 2	Write two blogs and publish one of them	Choose 1st subject and gather info	Write brief for supplier or prep the content internally	Post about blog
Week 3		Get testimonial for case study and write up article	Finalise material's content and design	Post testimonial from case study
Week 4	Finish and publish 2nd blog	Finish and publish case study	Finish and publish/ print material	Post about blog
Week 5	Send out newsletter		Contact recent customers to get feedback/ reviews	Post about new evergreen content
Week 6	Write two blogs and publish one of them	Choose 2nd subject and gather info	Review evergreen content/ auto-mations and plan updates	Post about blog

	Fortnightly blog and monthly newsletter	Publish one case study per month	Keep website up to date	Social media
Week 7		Get testimonial for case study and write up article	Refresh a piece of content	Post review from case study
Week 8	Finish and publish 2nd blog	Finish and publish case study	Refresh a piece of marketing automation	Post about blog
Week 9	Send out newsletter		Contact recent customers to get feedback/ reviews	Post case study or review
Week 10	Write two blogs and publish one of them	Choose 3rd subject and gather info	Review photos & images on website & update	Post about blog
Week 11		Get testimonial for case study and write up article	Review headlines/ messaging on website & update	Post review/ quote from case study
Week 12	Finish and publish 2nd blog	Finish and publish case study	Check all pages have calls to action and are SEO'd & updated	Post about blog

As a business grows from a one-person marketing department to a marketing team, the tasks on your rolling marketing plan will be the ones to delegate to the more junior members of the team. These tasks are the things that are tried and tested and so the tasks are much easier to brief someone on.

If you haven't already, write out your 90-day action plan and rolling 90-day plan and put it in a place you can refer to it regularly. I have mine on a white board above my monitor so it's always visible when I'm at my desk and I can quickly see what I need to do today. What are the tasks that you do on a regular basis? Consider for a moment what you do to support your marketing every day, every week, every month, every quarter and every year.

At this stage, you might have identified whether you're a big chunker or small chunker, whether you prefer sequencing or theming, and laid out all your plans... and suddenly the reality of actually implementing all this might sound like a lot of work for one person or a very small team. This is a good place to talk about some other crucial resources: the skills, roles and people that will help your business really thrive.

ASSESSING THE MARKETING SKILLS YOUR BUSINESS NEEDS

Understanding the marketing skills needed within your business is essential to creating an effective, scalable marketing function. To assess where you stand, start by reviewing the marketing activities in your buyer journey that you are already doing. List the different activities, such as social media, email campaigns, content creation, or search engine optimisation (SEO).

Next, evaluate who is responsible for these tasks and their proficiency in each area. Ask questions like:

- Are these activities delivering the results we need?
- Do we have the time and expertise to execute them effectively?

- Are there gaps where key marketing tasks aren't being addressed?

Once you've identified your strengths, it's time to focus on the gaps. These gaps fall into three categories: skills you can outsource, skills you can hire, or skills you may be able to build internally by upskilling people already in your team.

1. **Outsource Specialist Skills.**

Some areas, like web development, graphic design or PR, require specific, deep expertise and, for most small businesses, are best outsourced to professionals. These tasks are usually project-based or highly technical, making them cost-efficient to delegate. Tasks like digital advertising and SEO are also best outsourced because they require constant monitoring and a deep understanding of ever-changing algorithms and technologies. Staying up to date in these areas demands full-time focus, making them ideal for specialists who live and breathe this work every day.

2. **Hire Core Roles.**

For significant ongoing tasks that are critical to your business, like social media management, email marketing, or content creation, it may make sense to hire. Be clear on the skills you'll need from the outset and those you'll be able to train the new person in once they're in place. In the next part of this chapter I'll discuss the three roles in a marketing team and how to choose the level you need to hire at.

3. **Upskill Internally.**

If you don't have the requirement for a dedicated marketing hire and already have a team member with potential, invest in their training. Skills like analytics, social media management, content creation, or campaign management can often be developed with the right resources and added to another person's role, helping your business grow from within. If you go down this route, though, make sure the person you choose has time to add these additional tasks to their workload and understands that these tasks are to be prioritised alongside their current responsibilities.

By regularly assessing your marketing skills and addressing gaps strategically, you ensure your team can adapt to your business's evolving needs while driving consistent results.

BUILDING YOUR MARKETING TEAM

Building a marketing team starts with understanding the roles and skills needed at each stage of growth. There are three main roles that a mature marketing team needs.

The Junior Marketer

For many small businesses, the journey begins with a junior marketer, who takes on essential but foundational tasks to keep the marketing wheels turning. A junior marketer might start as an apprentice or with a few years of experience. They typically handle tasks like updating websites, managing social media posts, and creating content. As they gain confidence, their role can expand to include customer relationship management (CRM) software updates, email scheduling, and more.

Working under a marketing manager or business owner, junior marketers need training and mentoring to ensure their efforts align with broader goals. While apprentices can seem like a cost-effective choice, businesses often underestimate the resources needed to develop their skills. With the right support, however, a junior marketer can grow into a valuable team member, laying the foundation for your marketing success.

The Marketing Manager

At this stage, responsibilities shift toward managing projects, overseeing campaigns, and coordinating a team. The marketing manager ensures that day-to-day operations run smoothly while maintaining the quality and consistency of marketing outputs. A marketing manager should have good planning and implementation skills but may not have the strategic skills needed to create a comprehensive and effective marketing plan without support.

The Head of Marketing

The pinnacle of this journey is the head of marketing or chief marketing officer (CMO) role. This position involves creating and implementing marketing strategies that align with business goals, managing the marketing team, and ensuring a coherent brand message. In a small business, the head of marketing often wears many hats, balancing strategic vision with hands-on execution.

Many businesses begin building their marketing team from the ground up, starting with junior roles like an apprentice or marketing administrator and gradually working their way toward hiring a head of marketing. On the surface, this approach makes sense — after all, junior marketers can handle most of the day-to-day tasks that keep things moving. However, there's a common (and wildly flawed) assumption that a young person must be a marketing genius just because they once went viral on TikTok with a dodgy dance routine. They might have the potential to become a marketing genius one day, but the skills needed to drive real results don't start at the bottom. They work in the opposite direction.

Strategic expertise is the foundation of effective marketing, and that comes from experience. Without a clear strategy to guide them, even the most hardworking junior marketer will struggle to deliver measurable outcomes. It's like trying to build a house without a blueprint — no matter how skilled the builder, the final structure won't be stable.

However, if you can only hire one marketing person into your business then starting with an experienced marketer is an expensive option. Plus, there'll still be all the marketing administration to do and it doesn't make sense to pay an experienced marketer to do that when someone much more junior (and less expensive) could do these same tasks.

For many small businesses, then, a great option is to hire a junior marketer with a couple of years' experience and also have a freelance strategic consultant or fractional CMO to mentor them and ensure their work is aligned with the business's strategy. If you hire a good junior marketer and nurture and train them in this way, there's no reason they shouldn't eventually grow into Head of Marketing, steering your company's marketing strategy with measurable results.[1]

Another good configuration for a small business can be a marketing manager with a team of freelancers or agencies supporting them in specialist areas, plus a few hours a week of an office admin who can add content to the website, schedule social media posts and send pre-written emails to your list. Smaller businesses can also utilise agencies and freelancers if the business owner has the time and marketing expertise to manage them themselves.

While it's tempting to think you can just hire someone to "do the marketing" and figure things out as they go, the reality is that successful marketing starts with strategic direction and filters down. Only when this foundation is in place can a team — no matter its size — truly thrive.

———

---

1. This is what I did in my own business, and if you'd like to read the case study, you can find that at https://rosconkie.com/TheMarketingMachineResources.

END OF CHAPTER CHECKLIST

I have:

☐ Identified my chunking preferences.

☐ Created my 90-day marketing action plan.

☐ Created my rolling 90-day marketing plan.

☐ Assessed the skills I have available to me in-house and what I'll need to outsource.

CHAPTER 11
BUILDING MOMENTUM

ESTABLISHING A REGULAR MOT RHYTHM

No machine can keep running well without maintenance. Whether it's a car, a piece of engineering equipment, or your marketing machine, regular check-ups are essential to ensure everything is working efficiently. That's where the Marketing MOT comes in.[1]

A Marketing MOT is about stepping back from the day-to-day running of your business every quarter to review, reset, and realign your strategy. It's the time to make sure your marketing machine is still pointed in the right direction and running smoothly. And here's the important part: take this time regardless of whether you've ticked everything off your to-do list. It's not about what you have or haven't achieved; it's about what you've learned and what your top priorities are now.

Over the course of this book, we've explored the key components of building a marketing machine:

---

1. If you live outside the UK and are wondering what on Earth an MOT is, the term stands for the Ministry of Transport. It's an annual test to evaluate the safety and roadworthiness of vehicles to help improve road user safety.

1. Understanding your ideal customer and proposition.
2. Mapping and improving your buyer journey.
3. Measuring your results and using data to inform your decisions.
4. Aligning your marketing activity to your objectives.
5. Setting up systems and processes to keep things running smoothly.

The Marketing MOT ties all of this together. It's your opportunity to stop, look under the bonnet, and make adjustments to keep everything working as efficiently as possible.

WHY A REGULAR MARKETING MOT IS ESSENTIAL

Running a business is a fast-paced, never-ending to-do list. It's easy to get stuck in the weeds, chasing urgent tasks while neglecting the bigger picture. A regular Marketing MOT gives you the discipline and the space to step back, reflect, and plan. It ensures that you are:

- **Staying aligned with your customers**: your ideal customer persona might change over time as the market evolves, your business grows, or you gather new insights. Taking a step back allows you to reassess who your customers are, what they want, and how you can serve them better.
- **Reviewing and improving your buyer journey**: as you implement new marketing activities, your buyer journey will evolve. Regularly mapping it out ensures you're creating a seamless experience that aligns with your customers' needs and removes friction wherever possible.
- **Focusing on what works**: metrics matter. They tell you what's working, what isn't, and where you should focus your energy. Your Marketing MOT gives you the time to dive into your numbers, identify patterns, and make data-driven decisions.

- **Prioritising your efforts**: not all marketing tasks are created equal. A quarterly reset ensures that you're always working on the right things — the activities that will have the biggest impact on your objectives.

WHAT DOES A MARKETING MOT LOOK LIKE?

Here's a step-by-step guide to running your quarterly Marketing MOT. It doesn't have to take days or require elaborate preparation — we do ours in a couple of focused hours. The important thing is carving out the time and following a clear structure.

1. **Review Your Ideal Customer Persona:**
    - Is your ICP still accurate? Are you attracting the customers you want? Have you noticed any shifts in who is buying from you or engaging with your marketing? I recommend my clients start with a blank sheet of paper every quarter and write out their ICP as if they're doing it for the first time. Then go back and compare it with last quarter. When we do it this way, we're often surprised by how the ICP has subtly changed when we'd thought it had stayed the same.
    - Look at any new insights you've gathered over the past 90 days — feedback, questions, surveys, sales data, or anecdotal evidence should all feed into your ICP to improve its accuracy.
    - Consider what is currently going on for your customer. Think about the economic, political, regulatory, technological, environmental, social and seasonal influences on them right now.

2. **Review Your Proposition:**
    - Is your value proposition still clear and compelling to your ideal customer? Has anything changed in the market, your products/services, or your competitors that requires adjustment? Again, I like to start from a blank sheet of

paper as new things often come up when your thinking isn't being influenced by what you wrote last time.

3. **Map Your Current Buyer Journey:**
   - Now that you've implemented new strategies or activities, map your buyer journey as it stands today. Identify what's working well and where there are still gaps or friction points.
   - Ask yourself: are there any new opportunities to make the journey smoother, more enjoyable, or more effective? Go back through the 'Optimising Your Buyer Journey' chapter for ideas if you need to.

4. **Review Your Metrics:**
   - Go back to your objectives and review your key metrics. How did your marketing perform over the past quarter? What are the trends, and what insights can you take from the data?
   - Look at the bigger picture: are your resources (time, money, people) being allocated effectively?

5. **Set New Objectives**
   - Based on what you've learned, what do you want to achieve over the next 90 days? Be clear, realistic, and focused.
   - Remember: objectives should tie back to your overall strategy and move you closer to your long-term goals.

6. **Decide What Will Improve Your Buyer Journey**
   - Once you have your objectives, identify the marketing activities that will help you achieve them. Focus on what will make the biggest difference to your buyer journey.
   - Think strategically. What needs to happen at each stage of the journey to move customers forward? What gaps need to be addressed?

7. **Prioritise and Create Your 90-Day Action Plan**
   - Now it's time to prioritise. You can't do everything, so use the logical process I described in the last chapter to work out what will have the most impact and in what order to tackle your "marketing smorgasbord".
   - Build your next 90-day action plan. Keep it simple, clear, and achievable.

BUILDING THE HABIT OF REVIEW

As I've said, the Marketing MOT is not a one-off exercise; it's about creating a rhythm. Think of it as a quarterly habit that keeps your marketing machine running efficiently. Put it in the calendar and treat it as a non-negotiable part of your business operations.

One of the most valuable ways to ensure this habit sticks is to have someone hold you accountable. Accountability is often the missing ingredient in successful strategic planning. It's one thing to promise yourself you'll take the time to review; it's another to have someone in your corner, ensuring it happens.

This is one of the most valuable roles we play for our clients. By scheduling a quarterly strategic review and planning session in their diaries, we force them to stop working *in* their business for a few hours and focus *on* it. This dedicated time makes all the difference: it creates a moment to reflect, take stock, and plan with clarity and intention. Often, clients tell us they would never take this time if left to their own devices, but knowing the session is booked — and that someone is holding them to it — ensures it happens.

I'm only able to force myself to do this for my own business because I can't bear to tell clients to do this when I'm not doing it myself. If I didn't have the pressure of having to take my own advice then I'd never get this done! And when it doesn't happen, I lose momentum surprisingly quickly and end up drifting off course. I waste time doing activities that don't serve my goals, or I waste money on things that aren't actually working, because I haven't reviewed my metrics. Believe me, the only way to make sure your marketing remains efficient and effective is to regularly review, learn and set a plan.

Your marketing machine doesn't need to be perfect to be effective. It just needs to keep moving forward. The Marketing MOT helps you do exactly that — adjusting, improving, and prioritising as you go.

So, even if you haven't ticked off every item on your last action plan, take the time to review. Reflect on what you've achieved, what you've learned, and where you want to go next. By the end of the MOT, you'll have a clear and focused 90-day action plan to take you into the next quarter with confidence.

The Marketing MOT is your commitment to continuous improvement. It's how you keep your marketing machine running smoothly and ensure it delivers results, quarter after quarter.

KEEP BUILDING, KEEP GROWING

You've done it! You're taking control of your marketing like an absolute pro. You've done the thinking, built your machine, and put yourself in the driver's seat. That's no small feat.

But this isn't the end. It's just the start of something powerful.

Whether you've already started putting your marketing machine into action or you're gearing up to get moving, the key is momentum. No more guesswork, no more hoping for the best. Now, you're in control. Every 90-day plan you complete moves you forward. Lots of small improvements add up to big results.

So, take a moment. Recognise how far you've come. Then roll up your sleeves and get back to it — because the businesses that succeed aren't the ones that sit back and hope. They're the ones that keep going.

And now, that's you.

Go and make it happen.

———

END OF CHAPTER CHECKLIST

I have:

☐ Blocked time out of my diary in three months to do a full Marketing Machine MOT and create a new plan (and added a reminder to do the same on a recurring three-month basis).

☐ Put in place some accountability to keep me on track.

✓ Become a marketing engineer.

BOOSTERS

My name might be on the cover of this book, but writing it was far from a solo effort.

First, to my husband, Paul. Thank you for your endless support, your patience, and for holding the fort while I disappeared into writing mode. You are incredible (even if you'd prefer I didn't say it publicly).

To my kids — my biggest inspiration and my most persistent distractions. I wrote this book to show you that big dreams are possible when you stick with them and have a plan. Your "help" during the process was... let's call it creatively unhelpful, but I wouldn't change it for the world.

Katie Evans, you started as an apprentice and, four years later, you're running the business like an absolute boss. Your ideas, your energy, and your belief in what we're building have been game-changing — not just for the business but for me. This book would definitely not have happened without you.

Laura Gale, you've been the ultimate editor, coach, and compass. Thank you for making my words clearer, sharper, and better without ever letting me lose my voice.

Amperative — I love working with you. I throw you wild creative briefs like, "I want a graphic of a marketing machine that looks like Big Bertha", and you somehow translate that into genius every single time. Thank you for bringing my ideas to life.

To all my clients — past, present, and future — this book exists because of you. You've taught me so much about what's possible in business, and I hope this book gives something back to you in return. Thank you!

I also want to thank all the marketers who I've learnt from over my career — the authors of the books I've referenced, and the talented people who have blessed me with incredible lessons in marketing, business and life.

Above all, I'm grateful to God for being the ultimate teacher and guide throughout this journey.

And finally, to you — my reader. Whether we've worked together before or this is our first encounter, thank you for picking up this book. I hope it helps you build something extraordinary. Now, let's get to work.

THE MARKETING ENGINEER

Ros Conkie isn't your typical marketer. She's an engineer too, and she knows how to build systems that work.

Ros started out in mechanical engineering before spending the last 20+ years in marketing. Now, applying the problem-solving, system-building mindset she developed as an engineer, she's on a mission: to help small businesses create marketing strategies that actually work — strategies that are structured, measurable, and repeatable.

Having worked with a diverse range of companies, from business services and coaching, to robotics and medical devices, Ros has a unique ability to turn chaotic marketing into order and structure. Since 2012, she's been working independently as a consultant, trainer, and coach, equipping business owners with the clarity and confidence to take control of their marketing and drive real growth.

Based in Portishead, North Somerset, Ros is passionate about making marketing logical, achievable, and — most importantly — effective. Because when you have a solid plan, marketing stops being a gamble and starts being a reliable driver of business success.

For more information and updates:
rosconkie.com
For resources that accompany this book:
rosconkie.com/TheMarketingMachineResources

[in] linkedin.com/in/rosconkie
[▶] youtube.com/rosconkie

APPENDIX 1: MARKET RESEARCH

When you're not familiar enough with your audience to put together a detailed ideal customer persona and value proposition off the bat, a little bit of market research saves a lot of time and money. It doesn't have to be expensive or complicated; just enough to get some insights into what's going on in your customers' minds.

Step 1: Identify exactly what you want to learn

Go back through what you've done so far on your ideal customer persona and your value proposition, and put an asterisk next to the bits you're not confident in. What were the questions you particularly struggled to answer?

You might want to answer the question, "What's the most important problem we solve for our customers?" or you might want to ask, "What are all the problems we solve for our customers?" These are two different questions which may need slightly different approaches, so be as specific as you can.

Use this to formulate the kinds of questions you'll want to ask your audience.

Questions you might want to find out the answer to are things like:

- How much would our audience be willing to spend to solve X problem?
- What do our customers value most about what we do?
- What information do our customers want to have about our product before they buy?
- What reservations or concerns do our customers have about buying from a company like us?
- What are the implications of buying from us if their purchase doesn't deliver what it promises?

Be realistic here. It's easy to get carried away and think, "I want to find out every single thing about my customers!" If you find you have more than five or six questions, then prioritise them so you have a shortlist of the essential information you need to gather.

I also recommend thinking about a budget at this point, in terms of both time and money, so consider what this information is worth to you and set yourself a budget that you'd be comfortable investing in this research.

Step 2: Define who you'll ask

Hopefully you'll have a rough idea of the kinds of people you want to approach but try to be specific about it. If you want to speak to HR managers, for example, what size of company do you want to target? Do you want to speak to people who are new in their role or people who have been doing the job for a while?

Are you likely to get better information from people you've worked with before or with people who have never heard of you? This is often difficult to answer in advance. Depending on what you want to learn, it may be much easier to go out to your existing customers and ask how they felt about this question before they bought from you, rather than to ask this of people who haven't bought from you (since they may not consider the problem to be something that needs to be solved).

If you've chosen to go out to people who you haven't met before, write a persona for the person you'd like to speak to, including as much demographic information as possible, as this will help you to find them.

Step 3: Decide on the best research method and conduct your research

The method you choose will depend on what you'd like to learn, and who you're going to reach out to.

Before you dive into questionnaires and interviews, ask yourself if you might be able to find this information with some good old-fashioned desk research. Does Google or ChatGPT know the answer? Can discussions on Facebook or LinkedIn give you some insights into your audience's opinions and concerns?

If you can answer your questions using information that already exists, it'll save you a lot of time. And if it can't answer your question completely, it may help you partially answer your question before you go out to collect more specific information from your audience to fill in the blanks.

If Internet searching isn't enough to answer your question, then the next step is to go out to your market and gather your own information. Your method will depend on the information you want to gather.

If you're going out to existing customers to find out which of their top five pain points are the most important, then a questionnaire may be the best choice.

If you want to hear what words people in your audience would use to describe their situation before working with you, then an interview may be a better option.

Interviews

One of my favourite ways to get information about what people really think is to interview a small number of people. The great thing about interviews is that you can get really in-depth information about your audience and what's really going on in both their Chimp brain and their human brain. Because it's a conversation, you can explore unexpected tangents that come up, and often this is what gives you really valuable data about your customers.

Interviews can be formal or informal — if you have only a small number of questions to ask, then you may be able to do a larger number of short, informal interviews over the phone or video call. If you have a lot of information to gather then I'd make it more formal, arrange a specific time and place (face-to-face is best if you can), explain to them why you're asking these questions and how you'll use the data. Always make it clear you're curious to learn and build rapport first to make sure you're getting honest answers.

Always prepare your questions in advance to make sure they're clear and unbiased. Consider the kinds of answers you might get and prepare potential follow-up questions like, "And what do you think about that?" or, "What's the impact of that?" or just, "That's interesting, can you tell me more about that?"

If you've got a lot of questions, put the easy ones at the beginning so your interviewee can relax and stop overthinking their answers. Put your most important questions after these early "warm-up" questions to make sure you get answers to them, and leave the least important ones to the end (in case you run out of time, or your interviewee loses interest or you have to cut the interview short).

If possible, record the interviews so you can go back and listen again. Always thank your interviewees and make sure they know how appreciative you are. You might want to consider offering an appropriate incentive for taking part, although if they're customers that you have a good relationship with then I find that a thank-you gift afterwards is usually better. I've also had clients do interviews over lunch so the free lunch (in a nice restaurant!) is effectively an incentive and thank-you in one.

When I gather information from my customers I try to offer some help or advice in return, or if they've given me a lot of their time then I might give them a free strategy session or something similar to show my appreciation.

Interviews are such a great tool for gathering information, especially from existing customers who already have a relationship with you. You might find the first few challenging as it's a bit of a skill but keep practising and you'll get better. It's really worth it.

Focus groups

Another way to gather information is with focus groups, which is when you get a group of people from your audience in a room and ask them questions as a group. Focus groups are most useful during product development or when you're developing your proposition, as you can watch people's behaviour and listen to their conversations between themselves. Ask open questions to get discussions going — bringing some visual or physical materials can also help with this.

Here are some key situations where focus groups are particularly useful:

- **Understanding Group Dynamics:** if you want to see how potential customers influence each other's opinions or how they talk about your product in a social setting, a focus group gives you that opportunity.
- **Idea Generation and Concept Testing:** if you're developing a new product or service, a focus group lets you test ideas, features and prototypes with live feedback. Participants can build on each other's thoughts, which can give you much deeper insights.
- **Exploring Emotional Reactions:** watching people's body language and tone of voice can help you understand their true feelings about a product or message. This can be harder to capture in structured interviews.
- **Visual or Physical Stimuli Testing:** if your product is something tangible, like packaging or an ad campaign, a focus group lets you see how people, hold, open or physically react to it in real-time.

Focus groups do have limitations, however — you have to watch out for peer pressure influencing people's responses and dominant participants steering the conversation. If you're looking for deeper, unbiased individual insights, interviews might be better.

As with interviews, make sure you've prepared your questions in advance and have everything ready for your session. Remember to record the session so you can watch it back.

Surveys and questionnaires

A hugely popular method for gathering information is with surveys and questionnaires. There are plenty of tools online now, like SurveyMonkey and Google Forms, which make gathering data much easier.

Surveys can also give you quantitative information, so for example you might learn that one problem is significantly more important to customers than others, or you might learn that a number of problems are roughly of equal importance. Interviews and focus groups are less likely to give quantitative information like this because the sample sizes are usually too small to be statistically significant.

Depending on your budget, a comprehensive market research project could combine interviews and surveys. You might interview five or 10 customers to find out all the reasons people buy from you. Then you could use their answers in a survey to find out which of those reasons are most common among your whole audience. In this case, you might use questions like, "On a scale of 1 to 10, how do you rate the importance of the following concerns?"

Always have an "other" option with a text box for people to put new answers in, just in case your interviews haven't identified all the answers.

When doing a survey, think about how long it'll take people to answer it and whether they'll be prepared to spend that time giving you the information. Closed questions (like yes or no, or ticking boxes) take less time than open questions where they have to write or type their answers.

Make sure that you keep your questions concise and to the point. Avoid adding questions just because you think it might be interesting, because this will reduce your response rate. If you can, aim to keep it to three or four really specific and concise questions.

Think about how you can make it as easy as possible for people to complete it and consider offering a gift, a voucher or prize-draw to give people an extra incentive, especially if it's more than a couple of questions. Value people's time and be clear that you want honest answers — you don't want people to tell you what they think you want to hear just so they get the reward!

Keep your questions unbiased. Check this by asking yourself: can you tell what our opinion is from this question? If the questions give away your opinion then it's biased and you need to reword it, otherwise your data won't be accurate.

There's plenty of information online and in various books about survey design, so if you're spending a lot of time or money on surveys then it's probably worth reading up on it or considering outsourcing this to a market research agency.

Other methods

I mentioned searching on social media already, but you can also get useful marketing information by using polls, and by asking questions in groups. Asking a question in a group that your audience hangs out in is a bit like a focus group, so treat it like that. Ask the question, see what people say, and ask follow-up questions if your audience is friendly and helpful. Keep an attitude of unbiased curiosity and be careful with your wording to make sure you're not leading them one way or another.

In addition to the methods above, there are other ways to gather information such as customer feedback forms, online reviews, and even just observing people's behaviour, such as using A/B split tests (software that shows one version of your web page to half your audience and another version to the other half and seeing which converts better) or heat-map software, which tells you which areas of your website users pause on and read. Think about the information you need to gather and be creative about how you might be able to find out the answers.

Step 4: Evaluate your research data

Don't wait until you have all your results in. Start looking for patterns as soon as you have a few responses in, and look for any common themes or complaints that are starting to emerge. If you spot people aren't answering the questions the way you anticipated, consider rewording your questions and restarting the process. There's nothing more frustrating than waiting weeks for people to respond to questionnaires only to discover they hadn't really understood the question you were trying to ask, so the answers aren't useful.

Be sure to ask yourself:

- Do these results answer the question you set out to explore?
- What do the results mean for your business?
- Are they what you expected to see?
- What changes do you need to make to your current marketing strategy now?

APPENDIX 2: PRICING STRATEGIES

Setting the right price is one of the most important decisions small businesses make. It directly impacts your profitability, customer perception, and overall success. I could probably write a whole book just on pricing but, to get you started, let's explore the key pricing strategies that work in small businesses.

Cost-Based Pricing

For businesses that provide services, such as consultancies, a common pricing strategy is cost-based pricing. This method is straightforward: you calculate the total cost of delivering the service and then add a markup for profit. The primary advantage of cost-based pricing is that it ensures you cover your costs while generating profit, making it relatively simple to implement.

However, while this model can provide a solid foundation for pricing, it doesn't always take into account market conditions or customer willingness to pay. So, it's important to balance your costs with what your customers expect and are willing to pay. If your costs are high but the market won't support a price high enough to make a reasonable profit, you may need to adjust either your pricing or your cost structure.

Another challenge with cost-based pricing is that it doesn't emphasise the value you're providing to the customer. To avoid this pitfall, consider reviewing your pricing periodically and assessing whether the value you offer justifies your markup. If you find that your customers see your offering as higher value than what you're charging, you could gradually increase prices or shift towards a value-based model to reflect this. Alternatively, if the perceived value is lower than expected, you can work on enhancing your offering or changing how you communicate it to potential customers.

In short, while cost-based pricing provides a baseline for your rates, it's essential to ensure that it aligns with both the value you deliver and market expectations. Be prepared to adjust as your business grows and the market evolves.

Value-Based Pricing

Rather than setting prices based on what your competitors charge or simply what it costs you to produce the product or service, value-based pricing focuses on the perceived value to the customer. Ask yourself, what problem does your product or service solve? How much is that worth to your customer? This strategy works well if you offer a unique product or service that significantly improves the customer's life or business. By aligning your price with the value you provide, you avoid undervaluing your offering and can command higher prices.

I first heard the following story while studying engineering at university, and it's stuck with me ever since, because it's a perfect example of value-based pricing in action.

The story goes that Henry Ford was once called in to consult on a manufacturing issue at a factory. The company was losing millions of dollars because a critical piece of equipment was malfunctioning, and no one could figure out what was wrong. Ford arrived, spent a couple of hours walking around, listening, and observing the machinery. He eventually pulled out a piece of chalk, marked a single spot on a piece of equipment and said, "Replace this part, and your problem will be solved."

A few weeks later, Ford sent them the bill. It was for $10,000, which seemed steep given that it didn't take him long to identify the issue. The company, somewhat perplexed, asked for a breakdown of the charges. Ford's response was simple and revealing:

"Chalk: 50 cents. Knowing where to put the chalk: $9,999.50."

This story perfectly illustrates how value-based pricing works. Ford didn't charge for his time or the chalk he used. He charged for the immense value his expertise brought to the situation — he knew exactly where to focus his attention to fix the problem, and that saved the company millions of dollars.

Pricing strategies for new products and markets

If you're entering a competitive market or trying to attract customers quickly, penetration pricing might be a good fit. This strategy involves setting a low initial price to attract new customers, and once you've established a customer base, you gradually raise your prices. This approach can create buzz and encourage trials, but be careful — if you price too low, customers might perceive your offering as low quality, and you could struggle to increase prices later without backlash.

Price skimming is the opposite of penetration pricing. Price skimming involves setting a high initial price and then gradually lowering it over time. This is common for businesses with innovative products or services, where early adopters are willing to pay a premium.

Over time, as the novelty fades or competition increases, you lower the price to attract more price-sensitive customers. This approach can maximise profits at the start but requires a steady pipeline of customers willing to pay the lower price in order to remain sustainable.

Bundle Pricing

If you offer multiple products or services, bundle pricing can be an effective strategy. By packaging related items together at a lower price than if bought separately, you create an incentive for customers to buy more.

This not only boosts your average order value but also helps to increase perceived value, especially if the bundle offers significant savings.

Remaining competitive

In highly competitive markets, competitive pricing may be necessary to stay relevant. This strategy involves researching what your competitors are charging and adjusting your prices to be in line with theirs. While this can help you stay competitive, it's important to ensure that you're not underpricing your offerings or sacrificing your business's value in the process. It's essential to consider the less obvious but extremely valuable pieces you may be delivering, such as customer service and your expertise, when comparing with competitors.

Remember, pricing is an ongoing process. Continuously evaluate your pricing strategy based on customer feedback, market trends, and your own business goals. The key is to find a balance between attracting customers, maintaining profitability, and reflecting the true value of your offerings.

FURTHER READING

- **Start with Why** by Simon Sinek (how purpose-driven businesses inspire action and loyalty).
- **The Lean Startup** by Eric Ries (Agile methodology and iterative business development).
- **Made to Stick** by Chip Heath & Dan Heath (how to craft memorable marketing messages).
- **Building a StoryBrand** by Donald Miller (messaging and storytelling in marketing).
- **The Chimp Paradox** by Prof. Steve Peters (understanding the emotional and logical sides of decision-making).
- **To Sell is Human** by Daniel Pink (how sales — and by extension, marketing — is about influence, not pushiness).
- **Influence: The Psychology of Persuasion** by Robert Cialdini (understanding buyer psychology).
- **The Challenger Sale** by Matthew Dixon & Brent Adamson (strategic sales and marketing alignment).
- **The Leaky Funnel** by Hugh MacFarlane (aligning sales and marketing to fix gaps in the buyer journey).
- **Flip the Funnel** by Joseph Jaffe (why focusing on customer retention is more effective than endless lead generation).
- **Watertight Marketing** by Bryony Thomas (practical, strategic marketing for SMEs).
- **The Jelly Effect: How to Make Your Communication Stick** by Andy Bounds (practical strategies for making your messages clear, engaging, and memorable).
- **Time Mastery** by John McLachlan & Karen Meager (practical strategies for improving productivity and effectiveness).
- **They Ask, You Answer** by Marcus Sheridan (customer-focused content marketing).
- **This Is Marketing** by Seth Godin (marketing fundamentals with a human approach).
- **Obviously Awesome** by April Dunford (positioning and differentiation).
- **Purple Cow** by Seth Godin (standing out in a crowded market).
- **Hacking Growth** by Sean Ellis & Morgan Brown (growth marketing strategies).
- **Scientific Advertising** by Claude Hopkins (old-school but still brilliant on marketing fundamentals).

- **Oversubscribed** by Daniel Priestley (creating demand and making your business the obvious choice).
- **Pre-Suasion** by Robert Cialdini (how to prime customers to say "yes").
- **The Telephone Assassin** by Anthony Stears (how to use the phone effectively in sales and business development).
- **Don't Make Me Think** by Steve Krug (simple, intuitive design and user experience principles that apply to marketing).
- **Traction** by Gino Wickman (a structured system for growing and running a business effectively).
- **Fix This Next** by Mike Michalowicz (how to systematically identify and solve the biggest bottleneck in your business).
- **Create Demand, Not Leads** by Ajay Patel (a structured approach to demand generation, attracting high-value customers).

www.ingramcontent.com/pod-product-compliance
Lightning Source LLC
Chambersburg PA
CBHW041209220326
41597CB00030BA/5137